GOUACHE

STEP BY STEP ART SCHOOL
GOUACHE

JACK BUCHAN AND JONATHAN BAKER

HAMLYN

First published in Great Britain in 1993
by Hamlyn an imprint of Reed Consumer Books Limited
Michelin House, 81 Fulham Road, London SW3 6RB
and Auckland, Melbourne, Singapore and Toronto

Copyright © 1993 Reed International Books Limited

ISBN 0 600 57906 9

A CIP catalogue record for this book is available at the British Library

Produced, designed and typeset by
Blackjacks
30 Windsor Road
London W5 5PD

Separated by Toppan Printing Co (HK) Ltd, Hong Kong
Printed in Hong Kong by Mandarin Offset

For Blackjacks:
Artwork and demonstrations for:
Yorkshire Dales, Rooftops, Scene From Another World,
Leopard, CDs and The Bathers – Roy Ellsworth;
Sunflowers, French Fishing Boats, Egyptian Village,
Falcons, Tulips and Alice – Ian Sidaway
Photography by Paul Forrester
Edited by Patricia Seligman

Credits

pp2-3 Rafael Valls Gallery, London, Bridgeman Art Library Ltd, London; pp 10-11 Private collection,
Bridgeman Art Library Ltd, London, © Mrs S. Russell Flint; p12; *top* By courtesy of the Board of
Trustees of the V & A, London, Bridgeman Art Library Ltd, London; *bottom left* Rafael Valls Gallery,
London, Bridgeman Art Library Ltd, London; *bottom right* Victor Lownes Collection, London,
Bridgeman Art Library Ltd, London; p13 Private collection, Bridgeman Art Library Ltd, London;
p14 Tate Gallery, London, Bridgeman Art Library Ltd, London; p15 *top left* By courtesy of the Board of
Trustees of the V & A, London, Bridgeman Art Library Ltd, London; *top right* Private collection,
Bridgeman Art Library Ltd, London, © Mrs S. Russell Flint; *centre left* Museum of Fine Arts, Budapest,
Bridgeman Art Library Ltd, London; *bottom right* Goteborgs Konstmuseum, Sweden, Bridgeman Art
Library Ltd, London, © DACS 1993; p16 Museum of Fine Arts, Budapest, Bridgeman Art Library Ltd,
London; p17 *left* Private collection, Bridgeman Art Library Ltd, London, © DACS 1993; *top right* Private
collection, Bridgeman Art Library Ltd, London, © The estate of John Piper; *centre* University of
Liverpool Art Gallery & Collections, Bridgeman Art Library Ltd, London, © 1993 Bridget Riley,
courtesy of Karsten, Schubert Ltd, London; *bottom* © William Grandison; p23 & p25 Roy Ellsworth;
p62 © Luciano Mugnaini and Daniel Bellucci; p98 © Jonathan Scott; pp142-143 © William Grandison.

Every effort has been made to contact all copyright holders of illustrations
used in this book. If there are any omissions, we apologize in advance.

Special thanks go to Helen Barbour of Winsor & Newton for supplying
all the artist's paints and equipment.

Contents

Chapter 1	**Introduction**	10
	History of Gouache	12
Chapter 2	**First Things First**	18
	Choosing your Subject	20
	Planning Your Picture	22
	Understanding Colour	26
Chapter 3	**Equipment**	30
	Paints	32
	Supports	34
	Brushes	36
	Other Equipment	38
Chapter 4	**Techniques**	40
	Stretching Paper	42
	Diluting Paint	44
	Laying a Flat Wash	46
	Laying a Graded Wash	47
	Blending Two Colours	48
	Building up Tone by Overlaying Washes	49
	Wet-in-wet	50
	Wet-on-dry	52
	The Opacity of Gouache	53
	Creating Texture	54
	Other Techniques	55
Chapter 5	**Landscapes**	56
	Yorkshire Dales	58
	Sunflowers	62
Chapter 6	**Man-made Environments**	68
	French Fishing Boats	70
	Rooftops	76
Chapter 7	**Abstract**	84
	Egyptian Village	86
	Scene From Another World	92
Chapter 8	**Animals**	96
	Leopard	98
	Falcons	106
Chapter 9	**Still Life**	112
	Tulips	114
	CDs	118
Chapter 10	**The Human Figure**	126
	Alice	128
	The Bathers	134
	Index	140

Chapter 1
Introduction

Although gouache has been around since the early 11th-century and is still extensively used by thousands of artists worldwide, it is a medium which often seems to be neglected. This is mainly because people do not really know what it is – not even that it is a watercolour – and therefore have no comprehension of the results that it is capable of achieving.

In fact, it is one of the most versatile media around, allowing the artist to use a huge variety of styles and techniques. Although gouache is made in the same way as pure watercolour, it contains a proportion of chalk bound with gum arabic. This not only makes it thicker than pure watercolour but more opaque, which is perfect for laying large areas of flat colour or for creating paintings where rich, deep tones are required. Another advantage of gouache is that, due to its opacity, light colours can be painted over dark without any hint of the underlying colour showing through. In total contradiction, gouache may also be thinned down with water to give a translucency which is comparable to pure watercolour and can be used in the same way.

It is exactly because of its contradictory nature that there has never really been an 'age of gouache', or any artists specifically famous for painting with it. But, gouache has always been widely used since it was first discovered and, without a doubt, always will be.

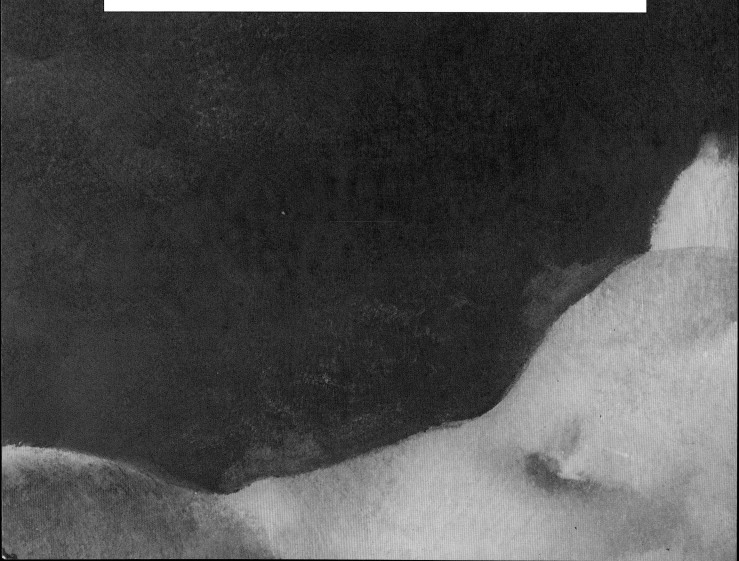

Introduction

HISTORY OF GOUACHE

The name of the actual person who first discovered gouache has not been passed down through history, but it is said that it was a monk who added zinc white to his watercolours whilst illustrating manuscripts. This created an opaqueness in the paint which – when used on the page for the illustrations – made his gold-leaf work stand out even more. Since 'gouache' comes from the Italian word *guazzo*, at least we can safely assume that its country of origin was Italy.

Even when gouache was first 'discovered', it was not hailed as 'the best medium yet' and no famous artists decided to use it extensively. Instead, it remained in the shadows (as it does even today) as another member of the watercolour family along with tempera. However this does not make it any less important and, although other media come in and out of fashion, gouache always remains a constant and frequently used paint – rather comparable to denim jeans in the world of fashion! This is mainly because gouache does not lend itself wholeheartedly to any

particular style or school of painting. It can be used like pure watercolour when it is diluted and, in its opaque form, will respond well to the techniques more commonly associated with oil painting.

It is because of gouache's versatile nature that so many painters throughout the history of art have

made use of it. This is especially true in Europe, but surprisingly it was not known in Great Britain before the 17th century. It was the French artist, Joseph Goupy (1689-1783), who decided to enlighten the British by introducing it, but once again gouache did not cause a great storm. However, it certainly influenced the English

watercolourist Paul Sandby (1725-1809), who took to using it frequently. Even so, he was never known for his works in gouache and always remained a watercolourist to his fans and critics alike.

To prove the point of gouache's constant popularity, we now mention some familiar names who have all enjoyed its individual properties: Albrecht Dürer (1471-1528), Nicholas Hilliard (1547-1619), Peter Paul Rubens (1577-1640), Sir Anthony Van Dyck (1599-1641), Nicolas Poussin (1594-1665), Edgar Degas (1834-1917), Egon Schiele (1890-1918), Pablo Picasso (1881-1973), Henry Moore (1898-1986) and Bridget Riley (1931-). These are but a few examples, so over the following pages we show the versatility of gouache more graphically with an interesting and enlightening 'gallery' of fine paintings.

4

1 *Mary Queen of Scots.*
Nicholas Hilliard (1547-1619) was the son of an Exeter goldsmith and one of the first English artists whose life was fully documented. He became famous for his miniature portraits with a style close to that of the French court.

2 *The Rape of Europa.*
Richard Van Orley (1663-1732) was the eldest son of the Belgian landscape painter Pieter Van Orley (1638-1708), who started to teach him to paint at an early age. Through his frequent visits to Italy he took to painting historical scenes in the Italian style and was obviously influenced by Gaspard Poussin (1615-75) and Francesco Albani (1578-1660).

3 *Erotic Indian Painting.*
This painting is from central India and is dated around the late 18th century. It shows the sitting posture for love and how the garlands that the couple exchanged have been set aside.

4 *Red Parrot.*
Jacques Barraband (1767-1809) was a French painter who specialized in any subjects with a natural history nature. The celebrated traveller, Le Vaillant, employed him to illustrate his writings on the parrots and other birds of Africa.

1 *Clerk Saunders.*
Sir Edward Burne-Jones (1833-1898) was originally a decorative artist who turned to painting under the influence of Dante Gabriel Rossetti (1828-1882). When he visited Italy initially in 1859 and again in 1862 he became strongly influenced by Sandro Botticelli (1445-1510) and Andrea Mantegna (1431-1506).

2 *The Challenge: A Bull in a Storm on a Moor.*
David Cox (1783-1859) was an English landscape painter who also wrote *A Treatise on Landscape Painting* and *Effect in Water-colours* in 1814 which influenced painters throughout the 19th century. His personal style was very free and he could definitely be judged as a forerunner to the French Impressionists.

3 *'Diana' Blue Harmony.*
Sir William Russell Flint (1880-1969) was a famous society watercolourist who frequently used gouache. He was particularly fond of painting females, especially Spanish gypsies.

4 *Composition.*
Theo Van Doesburg (1883-1931) was a Dutch painter and theoretician who was leader of the *De Stijl* movement, of which Piet Mondrian (1872-1944) was also a member. Doesburg ran a magazine of the same name and lectured at the Bauhaus in 1922.

2

3

4

5

5 *The Acrobat Family.*
Pablo Picasso (1881-1973) will
always be remembered for his
partnership – or 'marriage', as
he called it – with Georges
Braque (1882-1963). Together,
they were responsible for
developing Cubism. This new
school of thought was
influenced by Paul Cézanne
(1839-1906), who stressed the
structural elements latent in
nature and helped to promote
the idea that a painting could
be successful even if it was
totally independent of reality.

HISTORY OF GOUACHE

1 *Two Girls Embracing.*
Egon Schiele (1890-1918) was
an Austrian painter and
graphic designer who was
strongly influenced by Gustav
Klimt (1862-1918). His most
powerful paintings are his
male and female nudes which
express emotions from passion
to despair. His female nude
studies in particular are also
blatantly erotic.

2 *Study of a Tree.*
Graham Sutherland (1903-
1980) originally studied
graphic art from 1921 to 1926
and did not turn to painting
until 1935. Although his
paintings at this time were
mainly surrealistic, he went on
to paint a series of realistic
portraits and to design the
altar tapestry for Coventry
cathedral.

3 *Raglan Castle,*
   Monmouthshire.
John Piper (1903-) did not start
to study art until he was 25-
years-old, when he spent five
years at the Royal College and
the Slade in London. He was
strongly influenced by Fernand
Léger (1881-1955), Georges
Braque (1882-1963) and
Barbara Hepworth (1903-1975)
and was fascinated by
Surrealism and Cubism. He
was also a designer whose
most well-known commission
was the windows for
Coventry cathedral.

4 *Study for Ra.*
Bridget Riley (1931-) was
influenced by the futurist
painters Umberto Boccioni
(1882-1916) and Giacomo Balla
(1871-1958), as well as the
Color-field painters of America.
She became famous in the
1960s for her Op art paintings
and in 1968 won the
International Prize for Painting
at the Venice Biennale.

5 *Paris Match.*
William Grandison studied at
Edinburgh Art College and
specializes in commercial
illustration, especially of a
nostalgic nature. His work may
seem a little out of place here,
but this is because he is an
airbrush artist. Gouache is
widely used in airbrushing as
it is water-soluble and
therefore will not clog any of
the delicate mechanisms in the
equipment.

2

3

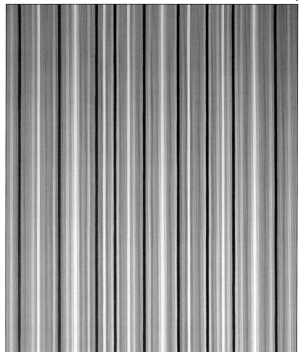

4

5

Chapter 2
First Things First

Before you can even pick up a brush, like any artist there are various aspects of picture-making you must first consider. In this chapter we look at these creative processes and then go on to examine the use of colour. You may think such theorizing to be a waste of time and decide to skip the chapter. Please do not. Without this knowledge it will be difficult to create a successful painting. If you are a natural rebel and fight against all 'rules', bear in mind that you will need to know what the 'rules' are in order to break them.

There are two fundamental stages that you must consider before you start to paint: choosing your subject and planning your picture. With the step-by-step projects in this book both of these steps have already been done for you, since their real aim is to show you how to approach different subjects and use the medium with confidence. However, once you are 'on your own' things will not be quite so straightforward.

Also of prime importance is the mixing and use of colour, so every artist should aim to develop their talents in this area. It is easy to take colour mixing for granted and then wonder why you have created a muddy mess on your palette.

Painting should always be fun, so we have tried not to labour the points too strongly. Read through this chapter and study its contents, but remember that at the end of the day your own preferences should dictate how you work.

First Things First

CHOOSING YOUR SUBJECT

The first stage of any painting is to select your subject. It is at this point that many beginner's minds go blank. There is something about an empty sheet of paper which seems magically to produce a complete mental block. The step-by-step projects in this book provide you with your first dozen paintings. If inspiration is lacking when you come to do your 13th masterpiece, then relax and try painting whatever is in front of you. It could be the view from your window, a pet, a close relative, an untidy bedroom. The subjects are all around just waiting for you to capture them in paint.

Magazines can be a great source of inspiration – we both go weak at the knees when we look in a travel brochure for an exotic holiday location! Advertisements can be particularly useful in setting off a train of thought. Once your brain starts whirring, who knows what painting you will eventually end up with.

It used to be traditional for artists to carry a sketchbook with them constantly. Anything that caught the eye would be jotted down, and then on a 'blank' day the sketchbook could be referred to for inspiration. Today, with the abundance of cheap cameras on the market, the photographic album has tended to replace the sketchbook. Many of the projects in this book use old photographs as their starting point. So, if you are particularly stuck, get out that old holiday album. Even if inspiration does not hit you, at least you will be amused by how you used to dress.

The three traditional subject areas are landscape, still life and the human figure. These can be further subdivided. For instance in this book we devote one chapter to natural landscapes and another to man-made environments. In addition to these main areas we have also given some space to painting animals and abstract work. You may choose to concentrate on one area but, before you do, make sure that you try your hand at all the projects in this book. This way you will not only experience a broad range of subjects, but also gain confidence with your painting whilst picking up tips along the way.

Eventually, you will find that what you decide to paint is usually dictated by your interests. So, if you enjoy the countryside, you will probably concentrate on rural landscapes; those who are into the technicalities of painting may well see still life as the most pleasing choice. Whilst anyone with a tendency to hallucinate would probably find that abstract painting suits them the best!

As you will soon discover when you take up painting, you start to see the world around you in a different way. Suddenly *everything* becomes the subject for a painting.

PLANNING YOUR PICTURE

People tend to assume that the creative process starts when you first place the brush on the paper. However, by this time many important decisions have already been made. Having selected your subject, there is the planning and design of the painting itself – usually referred to as the composition. The ancient Greek philosopher Plato said that "composition is the skill of finding and representing unity within diversity", which sums up the basic rule for any good composition. In other words, to be pleasing a picture should contain enough vitality to hold the viewer's interest. But that vitality must be organized and kept in check, otherwise the picture becomes meaningless. If you concentrate too much on the unity of a scene, it ends up looking monotonous and uninteresting; introduce too much diversity and the elements become scattered, each area attracting individual attention and so destroying the harmony. The skill is in finding the right point between anarchy and monotony.

Depending on the type of painting, you either compose the subject or the painting, and sometimes both. For instance, with a landscape you have little or no control over the subject but a number of decisions to make with regard to your painting. You have to decide on the view you will paint, how much you will include and what range of depth you will go for. You plan the painting rather than the subject. At the other end of the spectrum, with a still life you will need to decide on what you want to paint, how it is arranged, the background, the type and direction of lighting and the textures and colours present. You have complete control over your subject, so you only start painting once you have decided on the group's composition. You plan the subject in preference to the painting.

Traditionally paintings are rectangular – either as portrait (upright rectangle) or landscape (horizontal). Unfortunately, the human eye has a field of vision in the shape of an ellipse. Therefore a common problem for a beginner is being able to imagine their subject in a rectangle. In other words they have trouble defining the edges and deciding on whether it should be in the landscape or portrait format. An excellent way to overcome this is to cut out a rectangle from a piece of card. You can then hold the card in front of you, look through the hole and see the world as a rectangular painting.

Design

The design of virtually any successful painting can be broken down into a distinctive geometric shape which dominates the composition. It would seem that however complex a scene, if this underlying geometric pattern exists then the viewer unconsciously relates to this, exploring the painting along these compositional lines.

During the Renaissance period almost every aspect of a painting was planned out with mathematical accuracy. The artists of this period sought out classical compositional formulae such as the proportional division of a painting called the Golden Section (see diagram A). This

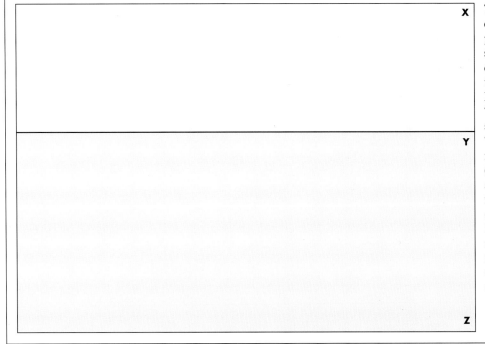

X

Y

Z

The golden section is the division of a line into two parts so that the ratio of the shorter length to the longer is equal to the ratio of the longer to the whole line. Here the line XZ has been split in this way. The ratio of XY to YZ is the same as the ratio of YZ to XZ. This ratio is roughly 8:13 or more precisely 1:1.61803398 (a calculator is recommended!) and when you draw a line out from point Y you will have divided the area at its horizontal golden section. A rectangle can be subdivided this way horizontally at the top or bottom, or vertically left or right.

DIAGRAM A

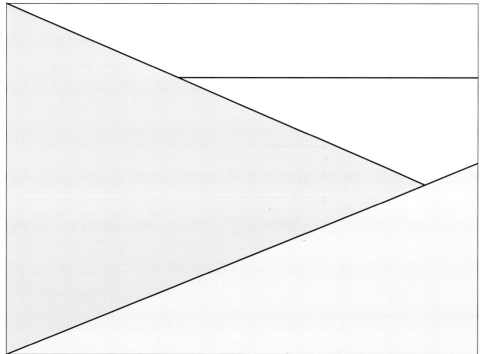

This gouache painting of a Greek valley by Roy Ellsworth clearly illustrates the principles of an underlying geometric design. As you can see from the diagram on the left, the composition of the picture is in fact dominated by two large triangles. However many flourishes – such as buildings or trees – the artist may have decided to add, the viewer will unconsciously relate to the geometric design, and so explore the painting along these lines.

PLANNING YOUR PICTURE

is a device for splitting up the picture space in what was considered the most interesting and pleasing way. The major elements in the painting could then be placed on the Golden Section – for instance in a painting of a landscape it would be preferable to have the horizon line falling on the horizontal golden section. Although modern artists rarely follow the golden section consciously, it is interesting to note how many paintings, when analyzed, do in fact conform to its rules, though by no means rigidly.

There is no need to get too embroiled in the use of geometric shapes and the golden section. But, if a particular composition does not seem to be working, try stepping back and giving the overall design further consideration. If no geometric underpattern is present, or if the golden section has been flagrantly broken, then this could be the root of the problem.

Viewpoint

With any painting the major influence is your choice of viewpoint. Whatever your subject matter – a landscape, portrait, still life – it is always a good idea to look at it from several different points before you begin to paint. For example, you may find that a still life

which looks uninteresting from a 'normal' viewpoint becomes much more exciting when viewed from one side or from slightly above.

The best viewpoint depends largely on what you want to achieve. For instance, an eye-level viewpoint is not normally used since it tends to flatten the group through lack of perspective, but it is a simple device in creating an unusual painting which will catch the viewer's eye. This element of the unexpected will promote an underlying tension not necessarily present in the objects themselves.

The perspective in your painting is dependent on your viewpoint. There are two basic types; parallel and oblique (see diagramsA and B), and

both are easy to master once you can identify the horizon line, your centre of vision and the vanishing point. The horizon line is always at eye level and is found by looking straight ahead. Your centre of vision lies on the horizon line in the middle of whatever direction you are looking. The vanishing point is the point on the horizon line at which all parallel lines that recede into the distance appear to converge (imagine standing in the middle of a long road with the sides of the road converging to a point on the horizon). With parallel perspective, the vanishing point will also be your centre of vision, whereas with oblique perspective there will be two vanishing points, one on either side of your centre of vision.

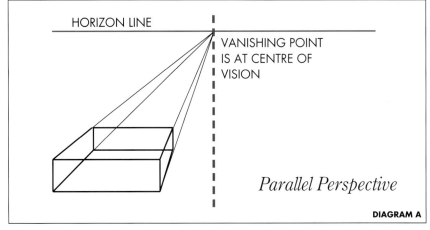

HORIZON LINE

VANISHING POINT IS AT CENTRE OF VISION

Parallel Perspective

DIAGRAM A

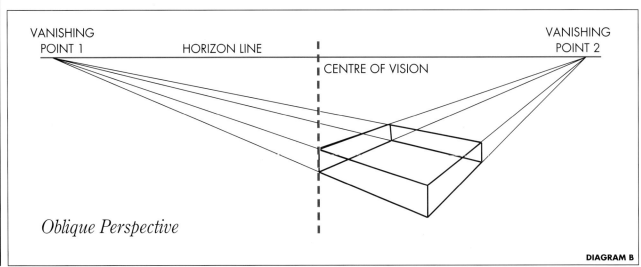

VANISHING POINT 1   HORIZON LINE   CENTRE OF VISION   VANISHING POINT 2

Oblique Perspective

DIAGRAM B

Due to the large paving slabs in this painting by Roy Ellsworth, it is relatively easy to discover his viewpoint and horizon line. You then realize that all the elements in the picture are shown in a perspective relating to this point.

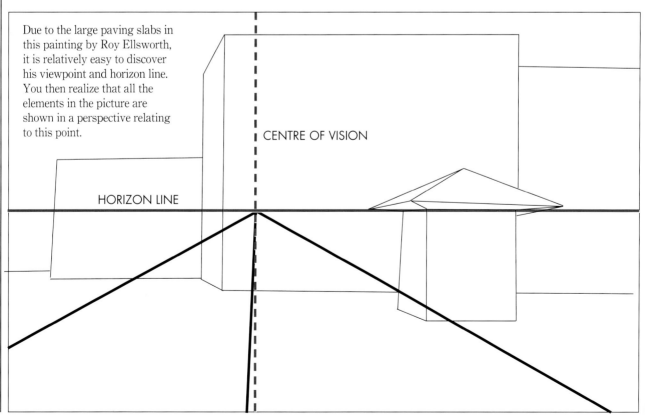

CENTRE OF VISION

HORIZON LINE

UNDERSTANDING COLOUR

To paint successfully with gouache, you must have an understanding of colour. Not only will it enable you to take full advantage of your palette, you will also avoid making elementary mistakes beginners often experience with mixing their paints.

It was in 1731 that the German theorist Le Blon discovered that a comprehensive range of colours could be obtained from just three primary colours: red, yellow and blue. In addition, the mixing of these colours gave rise to the secondary colours;

orange, green and violet. If you then increase the amount of one of the primary colours in the secondary colour mix, you will create a tertiary colour.

Unfortunately this is all very well on paper, but in practise the theory is flawed. You should be able to buy just three tubes of paint – a red, yellow and blue – and create every hue under the sun. You cannot. Although a particular red may create a perfect orange when mixed with yellow, when mixed with blue it is unlikely that you

will get a good violet. In truth, colours tend to lean in one direction or the other as it is impossible to create a pure red, yellow or blue. To overcome this problem you must split the three primary colours in half. For instance, instead of trying to use one red to create both orange and violet, use two: one red with a bias towards orange and one with a bias towards violet. This way, you can be sure that your mixes will work correctly. So instead of trying to buy three primary colours, you need to buy six. A good

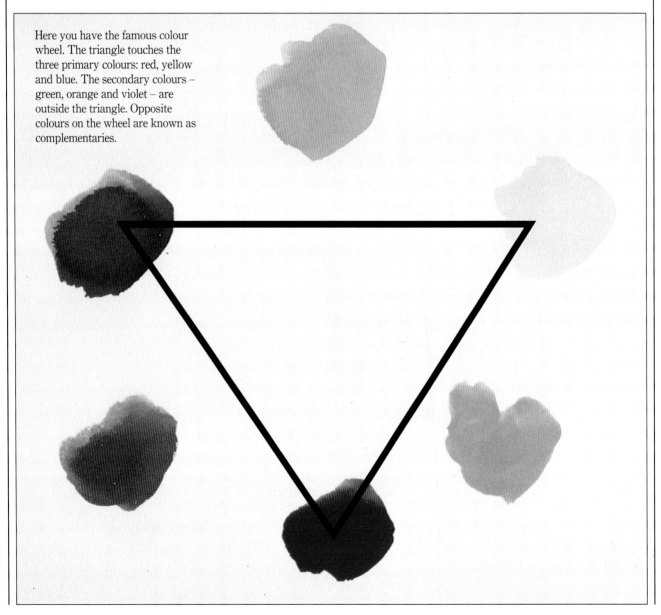

Here you have the famous colour wheel. The triangle touches the three primary colours: red, yellow and blue. The secondary colours – green, orange and violet – are outside the triangle. Opposite colours on the wheel are known as complementaries.

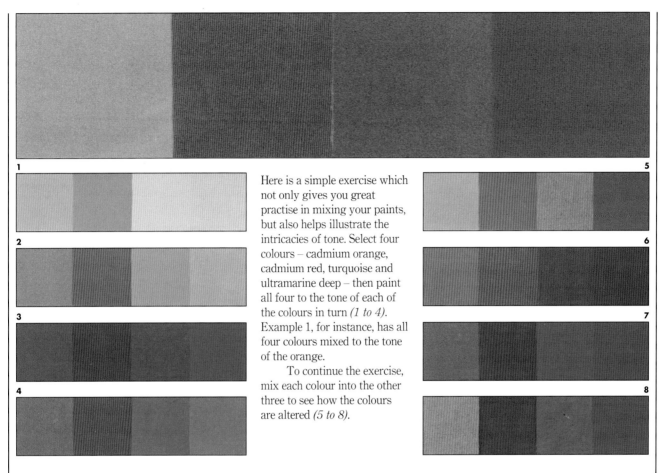

1

2

3

4

5

6

7

8

Here is a simple exercise which not only gives you great practise in mixing your paints, but also helps illustrate the intricacies of tone. Select four colours – cadmium orange, cadmium red, turquoise and ultramarine deep – then paint all four to the tone of each of the colours in turn *(1 to 4)*. Example 1, for instance, has all four colours mixed to the tone of the orange.

To continue the exercise, mix each colour into the other three to see how the colours are altered *(5 to 8)*.

recommended basic range would be cadmium red, alizarin crimson, ultra marine blue, cerulean blue, lemon yellow and cadmium yellow. From this selection you should be able to create virtually any hue you desire as long as you always mix the primary colours with the same bias, e.g. cerulean blue and lemon yellow both have a bias towards green.

You will notice that in some of the projects in this book a very limited palette was used – often with only three primary colours present. The reason for this is that when you use only a narrow range of paints you achieve a harmony of colour in the painting. In addition, even though a yellow and blue may not be creating a perfect green for instance, it will appear a suitable green in the context of the painting due to the colour harmony.

Complementary Colours

If you look again at our simple colour wheel you will see the red is opposite green, yellow is opposite violet and blue is opposite orange. These opposites are called complementary colours. To achieve full satisfaction with your painting, you must understand how these complementaries can help you.

When placed side by side, complementary colours accentuate each other, and this can be used to great effect in a painting. For example, if you have a landscape which contains a lot of green hues, then a red element placed within it will stand out dramatically. It was Paul Cézanne who first consciously juxtaposed certain colours to achieve this effect. He further found that by adding touches of one colour to an area of its complementary you could make the

main colour come alive. A good example of this would be to add dashes of red into an area of green foliage. Any flatness will disappear and the foliage will appear to shimmer.

You will also find that neutral tones can be easily created with complementary colours. If you mix together red and green you will create a brown, blue and orange create grey and so on. By varying the amounts of each complementary you can quickly create a whole range of these neutral colours.

By using the same principle, it is easy to tone down colours which are too bright and to create shadow tones. For the beginner this is a real bonus. So often blacks and dark greys are used to tone down colours or to create shadows, and so often this results in a muddy mess of a colour. If you have a

UNDERSTANDING COLOUR

red flower for instance, and you wish to paint in the shadow, then add green to your red. Since red and green are complementaries, the green will darken the red to a shadow tone.

Warm and Cold Colours

The colours of the spectrum can be split into warm and cold colours. All red and yellow tones are said to be warm because they remind us of fire. Blue and green tones remind us of ice so they are said to be cold.

You will find that the palette used for a painting is often restricted to either warm or cool colours, greatly affecting the mood of the painting. Cold colour schemes tend to give a rather harsh and atmospheric feel to a painting. Warm colours on the other hand tend to promote a feeling of well-being and contentment. J.M.W. Turner made evident use of warm and cold colour schemes in his paintings. Green and blue hues predominate in his

storm scenes, while his more serene paintings make use of gentle oranges and reds.

However, what you must remember is that no convention in art has to adhered to. For instance, if you want to create a painting with a great sense of vitality, one way to do this would be to introduce variety in the colours. A more subtle approach might involve using an overall warm colour scheme, but including one or two spots of cool colour to provide the 'punch'. As always, the trick to being a *truly* accomplished artist is knowing when to break or ignore the rules.

These two colour bars use the same principles we described on page 27. But instead of stopping after mixing each colour into the other three, continuing exercises, such as mixing in a fifth colour, were carried out.

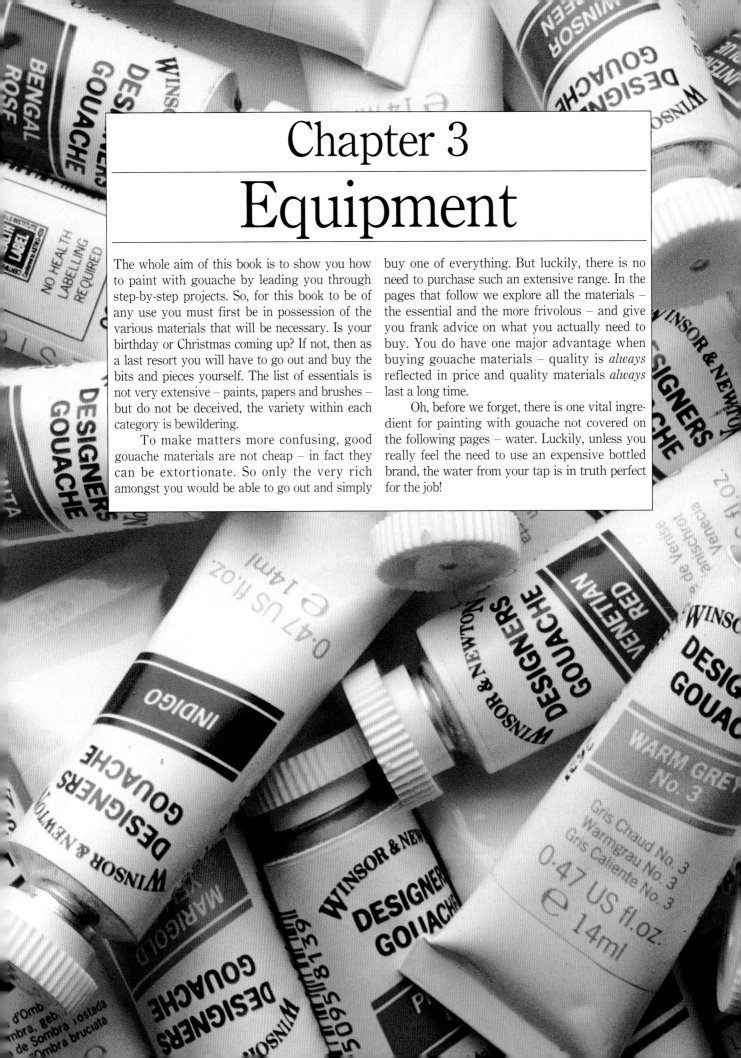

Chapter 3
Equipment

The whole aim of this book is to show you how to paint with gouache by leading you through step-by-step projects. So, for this book to be of any use you must first be in possession of the various materials that will be necessary. Is your birthday or Christmas coming up? If not, then as a last resort you will have to go out and buy the bits and pieces yourself. The list of essentials is not very extensive – paints, papers and brushes – but do not be deceived, the variety within each category is bewildering.

To make matters more confusing, good gouache materials are not cheap – in fact they can be extortionate. So only the very rich amongst you would be able to go out and simply buy one of everything. But luckily, there is no need to purchase such an extensive range. In the pages that follow we explore all the materials – the essential and the more frivolous – and give you frank advice on what you actually need to buy. You do have one major advantage when buying gouache materials – quality is *always* reflected in price and quality materials *always* last a long time.

Oh, before we forget, there is one vital ingredient for painting with gouache not covered on the following pages – water. Luckily, unless you really feel the need to use an expensive bottled brand, the water from your tap is in truth perfect for the job!

WINSOR & NEWTON

DESIGNERS GOUACHE

SCARL LAK

Laque Ecarlate
Scharlachlack
Laca Escarlata
Lacca scarlatta

14ml
0.47 US fl.oz.

PRIMARY YELLOW

DESIGNERS GOUACHE

LEMON YELLOW

Jaun
Zitr
Ama
G

Permanence AA

U.S.A. ONLY

NO HEALTH
LABELLING
REQUIRED

HEALTH
LABEL

0605 744

Made in England

DESIGNERS

PERMANENT GREEN LIGHT

WINSOR & NEWTON DESIGNERS GOUACHE

NERS ACHE

AP REEN

Verf de Vessie
Saftgrün
Verde Venga
Verde vescica

14ml
0.47 US fl.oz.

WINSOR & NEWTON

DESIGNERS GOUACHE

PRIMARY RED

Rouge Primaire
Grundrot
Rojo Prima
Rosso Prim

WINSOR & NEWTON

DESIGNERS
GOUACHE

ULTRAMARINE
DEEP

Outremer Foncé
Ultramarin, dunkel
Ultramar Oscuro

0·47 US fl.oz.

℮ 14ml

WINSOR & NEWT

DESIGNERS GOUACHE

SKY BLUE

Bleu Primaire
Grundblau
Azul Primario
Blu primario

14ml ℮

0·47 US fl.oz.

WINSOR & NEWTON

DESIGNERS

GERANIUM

WINSOR

DESI

GO

Equipment

PAINTS

Gouache is made from finely ground pigment which is mixed with distilled water and bound with gum. It is the inclusion of an inert white pigment – normally *blanc fixe* or precipitated chalk – that gives gouache its opaque quality. In addition, the reflectivity of the white pigment gives the main colour of the paint a greater vibrancy. However, gouache does have one major disadvantage, some of the colours are notorious for fading with time. The main manufacturers all produce colour swatches of their ranges, and detailed on these will be any colours which are noted for fading. You can then simply avoid these colours if you intend to paint for posterity.

Apart from the inert white pigment, the two most important components are the binder and the colour pigment. Gum is used as the binder since it is water-soluable and also increases the gloss and improves wetting. By far the most commonly used is gum arabic which is produced by several species of acacia trees found in Africa and North America. Gum tragacanth is also used occasionally, and this comes from a shrub which grows wild in Turkey and Greece.

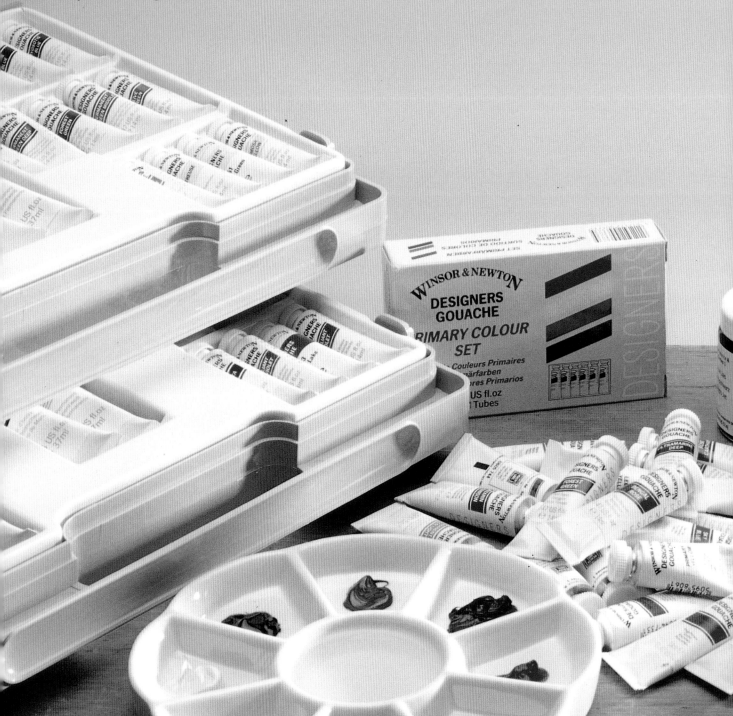

The pigments come from many different sources. Some occur naturally, whilst others are totally artificial. As we mentioned previously, some of these pigments fade with time. But this is not the only way in which they differ. Some colours are more opaque than others, a few are even totally transparent. They also differ in their staining qualities. Whereas a colour such as cobalt blue will not stain at all, cyprus green, for instance, will stain any colours painted on top of it. Again the manufacturers' charts should be consulted before purchasing paints since they will give you guidance on opacity and staining.

The most common form in which you buy gouache is in tubes, though you can buy certain well-used colours in larger pots. More recently, discs of solid colour have also been introduced which are rather similar to the pure watercolour variety found in children's painting boxes. The range of colours you can buy in tubes is vast to say the least. With the discs you have a more limited selection. But since gouache is so easy to mix, a small range of colours can be used to create virtually every colour under the sun. Perhaps the most confusing thing when buying gouache is the choice of different blacks and whites. Winsor and Newton, for instance, produce two different whites and three different blacks. However to make things easy, in this book we have stuck to ivory black and permanent white as these are the two most versatile. The tubes can be bought separately, but all the major manufacturers also sell sets which generally work out much better value for money.

As a beginner you should only need buy an introductory set which will contain nine or ten basic colours from which most of the spectrum can be mixed. As time goes by, you will probably find that certain other colours would be handy and these can then be purchased separately. If money is no object, then the sets go up in scale until you reach some which literally cost a fortune and contain so many colours that you might be persuaded that you would never have to mix any of your paints again.

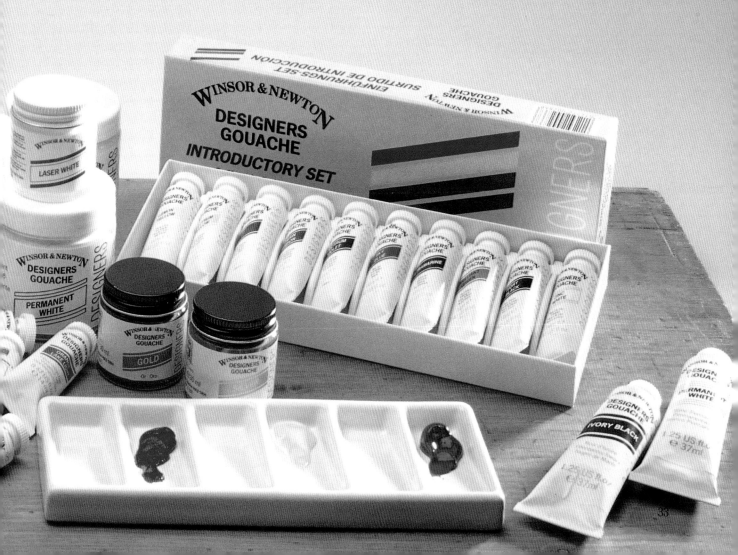

SUPPORTS

A support is any surface upon which an artist paints. With gouache, a greater variety of supports can be used than for almost any other medium. So long as the surface is free of grease or oil it will take gouache. Therefore cardboard, hardboard, wood and even material can be painted upon. However, the main support used with gouache is paper. This is lucky since it is cheap, readily available and highly portable. Any watercolour paper is ideal for gouache, but the range is bewildering. They vary in size, weight, colour, texture and the materials from which they are made. Most types are available in pads, but the larger sizes tend to come only as single sheets. As with most things in life, the more money you spend the better quality paper you will get.

The weight of watercolour paper is expressed either in pounds per ream (480 sheets) or grammes per square metre. Generally weights vary from the lightweight papers at 90lb (185gsm) right up to the very heaviest papers at 300lb (640gsm). The lighter papers will need to be stretched (see page 42), but once you get above 140lb (300gsm) this should not be required unless you are really going to be drenching the paper.

Since gouache is opaque, coloured papers can be used to great effect. In fact, as gouache contains white pigment any colours will actually stand out better on a tinted background. In this book we stick to working on white paper so that the projects stand out and are clear. Once you are working on your own, feel free to select tinted papers to work on, but remember to select colours which will complement what you intend to paint.

The surface texture of your paper is also very important. There are three recognized finishes: Hot Pressed (HP); NOT (sometimes called Cold Pressed or CP); and Rough. Hot Pressed has the smoothest surface because during its manufacture it is rolled between hot metal rollers which has the effect of ironing it. It is more suited to drawing, but many artists enjoy the unpredictable way the paint spreads across the smooth surface. NOT paper – so called because it is 'not' hot pressed – has a medium texture and is the most popular type. Rough, as its name implies, has a distinctly textured surface. Some artists believe that a grainy surface which drags at the brush is more satisfactory as it pulls the paint from the bristles. However, equally others would argue that a smooth surface is superior. The texture you choose is purely a matter for personal preference.

You can buy your papers in pads, blocks or as loose sheets. The pads are useful for taking out-and-about, but you must be careful not to use too much water. If you intend

doing a proper painting you must first remove a sheet and stretch it. The blocks have the paper bound around all four edges so they do not require stretching. Again they are very useful for working out of doors. There is a small gap that is not attached, so by slipping a blade in there and carefully working it around, you can remove a sheet once you have finished with it.

Watercolour papers can be made from a variety of materials. The most expensive are handmade from pure rag. However it is not really necessary to spend this much money. For the beginner, paper machine-made from a mixture of rag and wood pulp will be perfectly adequate. If you are feeling particularly adventurous try some handmade Egyptian papyrus for a journey into real decadence.

WINSOR & NEWTON

WINSOR & NEWTON

WINSOR & NEWTON

ARTISTS'
WATER COLOUR PAPER
Rough · 305 x 229 mm · 12 x 9 in
140 lb/300 gsm

Rough
Block of 15 sheets, 100% rag,
mould made, acid free water colour paper

Rauhkörnig
Block mit 15 Blättern, 100% Hadern,
gemachtes säurefreies Wasserfarbenpapier

Grain torchon
Bloc de 15 feuilles de papier aquarelle sans acide,
pur chiffon, fabriqué sur forme ronde

Grano grueso
Taco de 15 hojas papel para acuarela 100% papel de hilo,
hecho en molde, libre de ácidos

BRUSHES

If you walk into an art shop you will be dazzled by the huge selection of brushes available. Do not fear, because you will only need a small selection to start with. The most basic collection would consist of three brushes: a large one to lay washes, a medium-sized one for broad areas and a small one for detailing – although in truth a range of six or seven brushes is much more desirable, even for the beginner. The exact sizes you require would depend on your painting style and the scale in which you work.

By far the most useful brushes for gouache are the round type. These come in a huge range of sizes from 000 (the smallest) to 14 (the largest). However, for normal use you should not need anything smaller than a no. 1 or anything larger than a no. 8.

Artists' brushes are made from natural hair, natural bristle, synthetic fibre or a mixture of natural hair and synthetic fibres. Generally natural hair is the recommended choice for painting with gouache, however bristle brushes are very useful for applying the paint thickly for texturing or for the dry brush technique. Of the various types of bristle brushes, the one you should aim for are the Chinese hog hairs – normally taken from the Chunking, Hankow or Kynkeis hogs. Unlike hair, bristles are very hard-wearing and have an exceptional spring. Of the natural hair brushes the most suitable is sable. But it has one major drawback, it is exceptionally expensive. The hair is taken from the Asiatic mink or weasel, with the very finest known as Kolinsky (or sometimes Tobolsky) coming from the tail of the Siberian Mink. Pound for pound, this is more expensive than

gold! There are several reasons for sable being so popular: it comes to a perfect point; it returns to its original shape; it has an in-built springiness; and it holds and absorbs paint wonderfully. Other natural hairs are also to be found, such as squirrel, ox and camel (which in fact is often from ponies or squirrels but is *never* from camels). Often the less expensive brushes are a mixture of one of the above with a small amount of sable. The cheapest natural hair brushes are just made from the inferior hairs. Soft synthetic brushes can also be used with gouache, but be warned, although some are very good, others are really abysmal.

Brushes are expensive so it is important that you care for them properly. Make sure that you wash them thoroughly in warm water after use, ensuring that every trace of

pigment is removed right down to the ferrel (the metal band). Wipe the brushes with a soft cloth and gently reshape the hairs. Let them dry naturally, standing on their handles. Never leave your brushes standing on their hairs.

In conclusion, we really must recommend that you try to spend as much money as possible on your brushes. Although buying sable brushes will quickly empty the cash from your pockets, if you care for them properly they will last you a life-time. If you can afford it, we recommend the Series 7 range of pure sable brushes from Winsor and Newton. The middle-priced choice would have to be the Sceptre Gold range, which is sable mixed with polyester. Of the cheap synthetic brushes, the Cotman range has to be the best buy.

OTHER EQUIPMENT

The one last vital piece of equipment before you can start painting is a palette. They are normally made of plastic or ceramic and come in a bewildering array of shapes and sizes. Normally they are white so that the true colour of the paint is evident. Especially useful for gouache are the palettes which have a row of small and a row of large hollows. Paint is squeezed into the smaller hollows and can be moved as required to the larger ones for mixing or diluting. The round palettes are very handy for mixing colours, and the large dishes are designed for mixing up washes. Although ceramic palettes are normally more expensive than the plastic variety, their only real advantage is that they look nicer! In reality, ordinary household saucers and old plastic yogurt pots will do the job just as well, so we would advise you to make your own palette and put the money towards brushes instead.

There are a few other bits and pieces you can collect together to help you. Some are especially useful, the rest are more on the frivolous side.

A selection of graphite pencils (more commonly called 'lead' pencils) will prove invaluable. You will not only use them to plot your paintings, but they are also very handy for adding additional detailing on top of the paint. Also on the list of 'essentials' is a drawing board. Many techniques require the support to be moved or tilted to control the flow of the paint, and this is only really possible when the work is attached to a solid base. You will also need it to be able to stretch your paper (see page 42).

Less essential, but still worthwhile is a table easel. Obviously, due to the nature of gouache, you cannot work on a vertical easel. Therefore you are normally limited to working flat on a table-top. A table easel, as its name implies, is a small wooden easel which sits on top of your table. It has a simple slant adjustment which allows you to work flat or at a number of different angles, depending on what stage your painting is at.

Finally, one of the most essential ingredients when working with gouache is water. Normally you would have your water in an old jar or mug, so it was inevitable that someone would try to improve on this. Winsor and Newton now sell a non-spill water pot which is cleverly designed to prevent spillage even if it is knocked over. What will they think of next?

Chapter 4
Techniques

Gouache is one of the most versatile mediums of all, and will provide a lifetime's enjoyment. However, before you attempt any of the step-by-step projects provided for you in this book, you must understand the various techniques used.

Since gouache is a watercolour, many of the techniques are the same as for pure watercolour. Therefore, if you have experience of gouache's more well-known relative you should be able to speed through the following pages. But be warned, do not ignore this chapter altogether. Even the most experienced artist can improve themselves by reappraising the way in which they work, and in addition, the section on painting opaque will be new even to you.

For the raw beginners to the world of painting amongst you, then this chapter is probably the most important in the book. At first glance gouache may appear to be one of the easiest painting mediums to use. There are no messy oil paints to clog up your brushes and no waiting for hours as a layer of paint dries. But – and it is a *big* but – when you are working with heavily diluted paint even the most experienced artist would be hard pressed to predict the exact finished result. If you practise the following techniques thoroughly – and a lot of spare paper is recommended! – you will understand how to use the paint. Gouache's unpredictability then becomes half of the fun.

Techniques

STRETCHING PAPER

Although gouache is renowned for its ability to be used as pure, opaque pigment, a certain amount of diluted colour will always be used in a painting. Paper absorbs water which causes it to stretch, and, consequently, it shrinks as it dries out. Unfortunately, paper rarely dries flat, instead it buckles and wrinkles which in turn ruins your finished painting. The way to overcome this problem is to pre-stretch your paper. You can buy ready-stretched paper, but you will pay a premium for it. Stretching your own is so quick and easy that the ready-stretched does seem to be an invitation to be extravagant and lazy at the same time.

To start with, collect together the various bits and pieces that you will need *(1)*: a drawing board, a bowl of clean water, a sponge kept for the purpose, some gummed paper and, of course, a sheet of watercolour paper. Tear off a strip of gummed paper for all four sides of the paper, allowing a few extra inches on each to be safe.

Lay the paper on the flat board and fill the sponge with water. Then squeeze the sponge over the centre of the paper *(2)* so that you create a large puddle of water.

Now use the sponge to gently spread the water all over the paper *(3)*. The idea is to get the paper well dampened, rather than soaking wet, as this could easily damage it. If the paper is fairly thin you should only need to dampen one side of it. However, for the heavier papers you will need to carefully turn them over and then wet the other side in the same way.

Re-dampen the sponge, and run each strip of gummed paper along it *(4)* so that it becomes sticky. You can try licking them but, be warned, you will probably feel very ill afterwards. Whilst you are wetting the gummed paper, your watercolour paper will be absorbing all the water you laid across it and quietly stretching behind your back.

Lay the gummed strips along the side of the paper, overlapping them onto the board, and then run along

1

2

each of them with the damp sponge *(5)*, pushing down as you go. Make sure the paper is flat, doing the opposite side first so that you can gently pull out any obvious wrinkles. You do not need to use any force since the drying and contracting of the paper into a set shape will be enough to flatten it.

Allow the paper to dry naturally overnight and, when you return the next day, you will have a beautifully flat sheet *(6)* just waiting for you to paint upon.

3

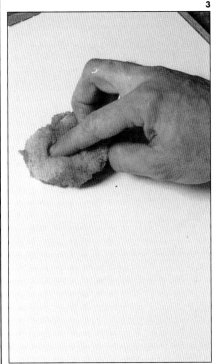

4

5

6

DILUTING PAINT

You will find that the more water you add to gouache, the more dilute the paint becomes. Since less pigment is present in the resulting mix, the colour appears lighter. So, rather than adding black to darken a mix or white to lighten it, you should be able to start with a partially dilute mid-tone and lighten or darken it simply by adjusting the amount of water present. In addition, if you are to paint with confidence, you must know what range of tones you can get from a particular colour, and how much water is required to get them.

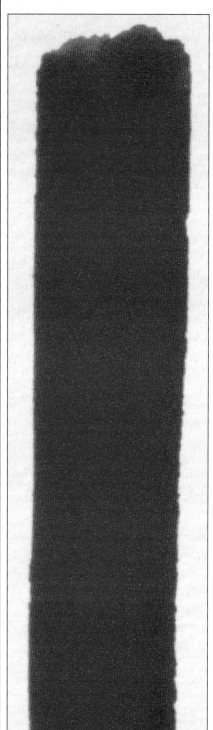  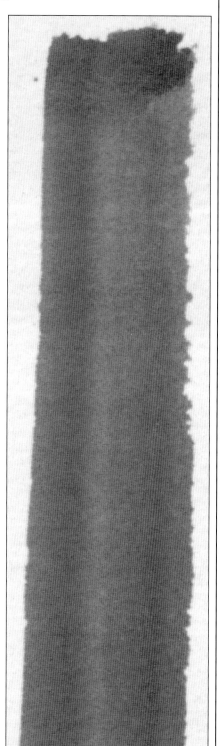

Start by painting a simple band with a large soft brush loaded with pure gouache paint. Add a small amount of water and paint a second band below it. Continue this process, adding a little more water at each stage until you get a band which is barely visible it is so diluted. You can then repeat this process with all your favourite colours, or experiment by mixing them together. By doing this you not only gain confidence with diluting paints, but also build up a valuable reference of colour charts for yourself.

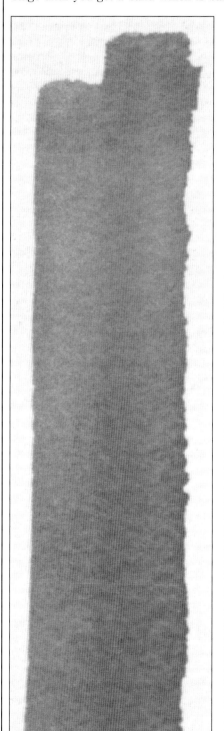

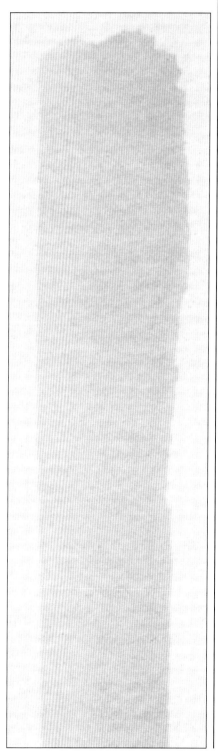

LAYING A FLAT WASH

One of the most important techniques when working with any type of watercolour is that of laying a flat wash. For a wash you dilute the gouache with enough water to make it fluid and then apply it to the paper to create a subtle and transparent layer of paint. The amount of water you add is tricky, slightly different to pure watercolour painting, and so requires a bit of practise. Because of the large amounts of water involved, it is essential that you have carefully stretched your paper beforehand or it will buckle which causes pools of colour to collect, making it impossible to lay an even wash.

The first step is to collect together your paints, a large brush, a jar of water, a dish and your pre-stretched paper attached to a board. Then mix your chosen colour with plenty of water in the dish, making sure that you prepare a sufficient amount to cover the area that you are painting. This is essential as, if you run out half-way through, you will have to stop to mix more. Not only will it be difficult to exactly match your original colour, but whilst you are mixing, the first half will have dried out, making it extremely difficult to add the second half without an unsightly tidemark.

Load a large soft brush with plenty of paint and lay it in long, even strokes across the paper *(1)*, starting at the top. Tilt the board towards you so that the colour pools at the bottom edge. Lay each stroke in opposite directions, picking up excess paint from the previous band as you go.

The secret is to work quickly, always making sure that the bottom edge remains wet. If you need to reload your brush with paint, do so at the end of a stroke. When you have covered the whole area, pick up any excess paint with a dry brush *(2)* or a piece of tissue, before leaving it to dry. You must keep the board tilted to avoid the paint flowing backwards so causing the wash to dry unevenly.

When the wash has dried, you will notice that the colour is much lighter than when it was wet. This is characteristic of gouache, and is something you must learn to allow for. If your wash is uneven, practise until you can get it right. Even though you may never want to lay a flat wash, it will teach you an essential lesson in control.

1

2

LAYING A GRADED WASH

Once you have mastered the flat wash, it is just a simple progression onto the graded wash. Here you have a wash of colour which starts as a dark tone and gradually fades away until it merges into the paper.

As with the flat wash collect together your paints, brush, dish, jar of water and stretched paper (attached to a board) first. Mix your chosen colour with some water in a dish and keep the jar of clean water next to it. Load a large brush with the full-strength mixture and lay a couple of bands of colour horizontally across the top of the paper. Tilt the board towards you so that the paint collects at the bottom of each band. Lay each stroke in opposite directions, picking up the excess paint from the previous band as you go.

Once you have laid a few bands, dip your brush into the clean water before you load more paint and lay the next band underneath, again picking up the wet front. Continue in this way, gradually increasing the ratio of water to paint, until the paint fades into the colour of the paper and you have a beautiful gradation of tone from top to bottom.

BLENDING TWO COLOURS

There are many ways to blend your colours, the best is to let the paint do the job for you. Two areas of dilute gouache painted next to each other will blend together naturally to create a smooth transition of colour.

Start by laying a flat wash of one colour *(1)* as explained previously, tilting the board towards you so that paint collects along the bottom edge. Then dilute a second colour and lay a broad band a little below the first wash.

Instead of working down with your strokes, go up so that you pull the second colour into the first a little way *(2)*. You can then work this second wash downwards as normal *(3)* until you have covered the desired area. Since the first wash is still wet, it will creep down into the second wash, the colours blending as it goes. The degree of blending that takes place depends on the amount of water you put into the two washes.

1

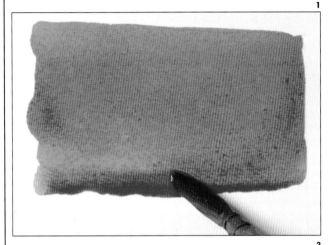

2

3

BUILDING UP TONE BY OVERLAYING WASHES

Although you have already seen how you can create a range of tones simply by adjusting the amount of water in your mixes, this is not the only method you have at your disposal. Obviously you could add white and black to lighten or darken your mix, but gouache is notoriously bad at retaining its colour integrity when altered in this way. Black in particular often deadens the colour so much that it just cannot be used. Other dark colours can be added successfully to darken a mix, but in many cases the simplest method is to build up tone by overlaying thin washes of the same colour. This process is used to great effect in many of the projects in this book, so it is vital that you follow this exercise closely.

Refer back to page 46 and lay three flat washes in a single colour next to each other. Make sure you mix sufficient colour to complete this exercise (six full washes). Allow the first washes to dry. Once they have dried load your large brush with the same colour and lay another wash over two of your initial washes. Remember to work in alternate bands, picking up the colour as you go. Stop and also allow these washes to dry. Finally, lay a final wash over one of the patches which has already had two washes. Once this has dried you will see that you have achieved three distinct tones *(1, 2 and 3)* of the same colour from a single dilution of a mix.

WET-IN-WET

Wet-in-wet describes the technique of laying one colour over another before the underlying paint has dried. This can create some interesting results as the second colour will bleed and merge into the first and enlarge the marks made. This is an especially unpredictable technique and very much depends on the dilution of the paint. However much practise you have, you will be unlikely to know what the finished result will be. But this is half the fun.

Painting Wet-in-wet

Wet-in-wet can be used in many different ways, but the most common is to paint directly on top of still wet paint. For example, lay a flat wash in one colour and, whilst it is still wet, paint a second colour over the top. Before your very eyes the second colour will spread out into the underlying wash, the colours blending as it goes. Although the mark of the brush enlarges dramatically and the edges blur, the basic form of your brush marks will remain. You will find that you can vary the extent of the blending and blurring by the amount of water you add to your mix.

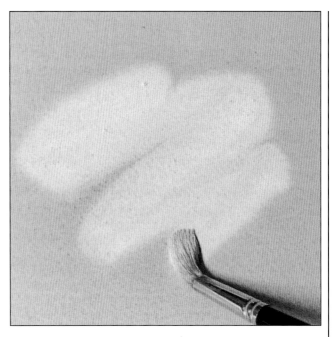

Dropping Wet-into-wet

Again lay a flat wash of colour (see page 46 for detailed instructions) and load a second large, soft brush with another colour. Hold the tip of the brush over the still-wet wash and tap it so that drops of colour fall from it *(1)*. These drops will immediately start to spread *(2)* merging slightly with the undercolour, but mostly pushing it away to create a halo around them. This can be a dark or light halo depending on the colour used. Allow the area to dry and then return to it. In this example the dark halo of green around the red drops is now very evident *(3)*. Not only that, but within the red patches there is a gradation of tone, from dark in their centres to very pale where they meet the green.

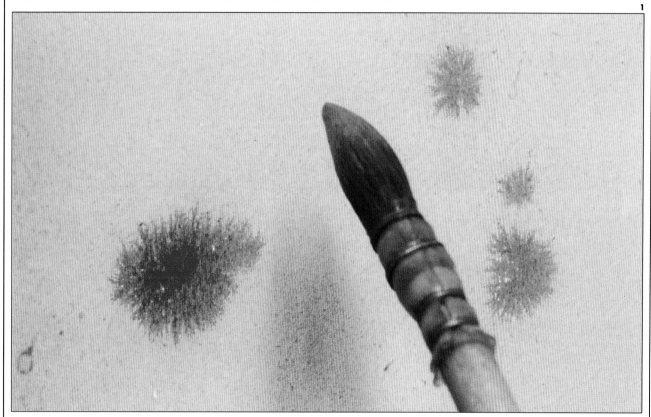

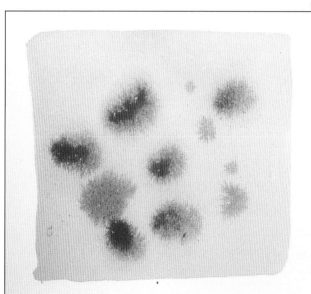

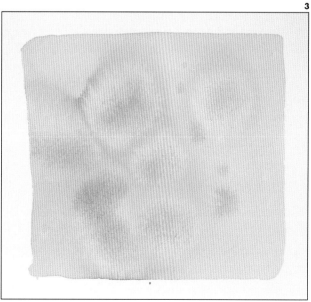

WET-ON-DRY

This technique involves waiting for the first colour to dry completely before laying another colour over the top and gives you a very different effect than wet-in-wet. This technique is used when you want to be able to control the overlying paint, keeping its form as applied, its colour and opacity. With gouache this is an especially important technique since you will need it to paint opaque highlights successfully (as explained opposite). In addition tone can be built up by overlaying the same colour (see page 49).

The application we show here is perhaps one of wet-on-dry's most common uses. Once an application of gouache has dried, you can paint another colour on top. Not only will it retain its colour, but it will have a lovely crisp outline. This allows you almost limitless freedom with your painting. For instance, you could quickly paint some rolling hills, allow them to dry, and then return to include buildings, trees, hedges, etc over the top – so building a scene up from the basic landscape rather than

having to plan your painting from light to dark as with watercolour.

To illustrate the point, lay a flat wash of a single colour and allow it to dry completely. You must make sure that the first wash is absolutely dry before you continue. Load a brush with a second colour and paint a rough swirl across the wash. You will notice that the second colour does not spread and it maintains its painted form with crisply defined edges.

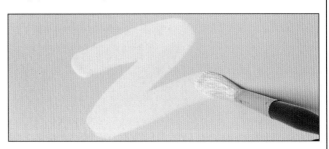

THE OPACITY OF GOUACHE

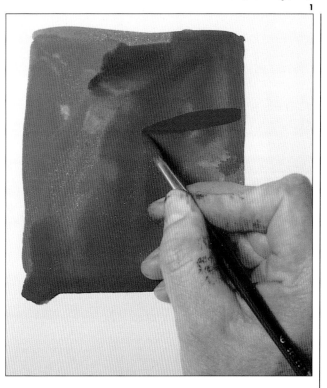

The major advantage that gouache has over pure water-colour is its opaque quality. This opacity allows you to paint light colours over dark which is especially useful for adding highlights. You will soon notice that the colours vary in opacity. The main manufacturers classify their colours in degrees of opacity. Winsor and Newton, for example, have four levels. This even applies to the whites available: permanent white has a maximum degree of opacity; zinc white is not so opaque.

To illustrate this opacity lay down a dark base area of colour and allow it to dry. Start by painting a bright colour, such as cadmium red, over the top *(1)*, making sure that the paint is not too wet. You will see that it does not blend with the base colour at all. Now paint a strip of titanium white so that it runs into the red *(2)*. As before, the white will not mix with the base tone. However it will mix with the still wet red. Due to its opacity, the base tone will not even show through the white, nor affect its tones in any way. Finally, add some yellow to the white so that you have a very pale tone, and paint further lines over the base tone *(3)*. Even when you mix together different colours, gouache's opaque quality is not lost, so this pale tone again completely covers the background tone.

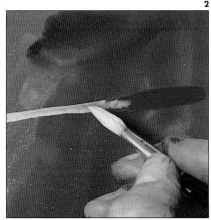

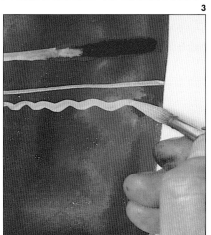

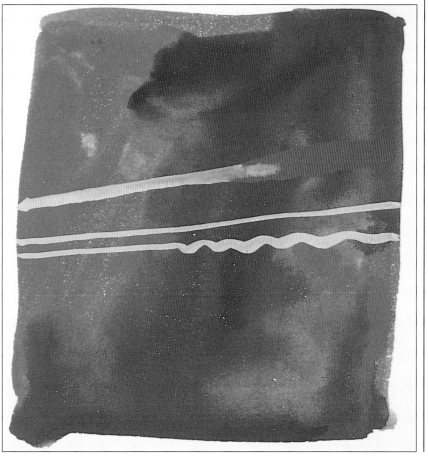

CREATING TEXTURE

The range of different textures you can achieve with gouache is only really limited by your imagination. Since you can paint it quite thickly you can add artificial texture into the still-wet paint with, say, an old, clean tooth brush, summer leaves, your fingers – in fact virtually anything you can think of. In this example, we concentrate on dabbing the paint with some tissue to create an effect rather similar to rag-rolling.

Start by painting a rough area for you to work on *(1)*. Use a couple of different colours to make it more interesting, merging them on the paper with your brush. Remember to lay the paint almost neat so that it is as thick as possible. Whilst the paint is still wet, bunch up some tissue to create a wad and press it randomly into the paint *(2)*. The tissue will lift off some of the paint, but not all, creating light patches from the folds and creases of the tissue. Stand back from this and you will see what a subtle area of texture you have created which could be used as a background to a portrait, for clothing or as a small part of a landscape – the possibilities are infinite.

Dry Brushing

Dry brushing is a simple technique which can be used to great effect. As the name suggests, it involves painting with a brush which is only slightly wet with paint. However, since gouache can be painted neat from the tube, simply omitting water will not necessarily give you the desired result.

First, lay yourself a flat base tone and allow it to dry. Load your brush, preferably a bristle, with a little paint, adding a touch of water if you need to. Work the paint well into your brush on the palette. If there is any excess paint 'blot' it off on a piece of tissue. Now simply pull the brush across the base tone. Since the paint is almost neat it is sticky, and this causes it to catch the rough surface of the paper and express the individual hairs of the brush in a random manner. As you can see in this example, not enough paint was blotted off the brush for the first few strokes since they start with a fairly solid band of colour, before tailing off into more broken patches. This technique is perfect for adding rough texture in a painting, and could be used effectively to suggest many different things, including grass, wintry trees and fur.

Brush Ruling

Due to gouache's opacity, highlights can be added in the finishing stages of a painting. If these are to be fine straight lines, as you might find on polished metal, glass and other man-made objects, then it is important that you get them perfect. Here the technique of brush ruling can be useful. However, this is not the only use it can be put to – it is also perfect for defining solid areas.

Simply place the ruler down where you want to paint your line. Lift its leading edge up so that the ruler is tilted and with the tip of the brush on the paper and the ferrel (the metal band) of your brush resting on the edge of the ruler, run the brush along, keeping your grip as relaxed as possible. So long as you hold the ruler rigid you will get a perfectly neat and straight line. By altering the pressure on the brush, you can vary the width of your line. To define a solid area of colour, paint two lines and, working quickly before they dry, carefully fill in the gap between them.

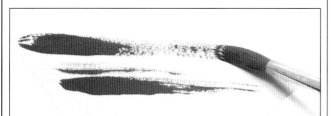

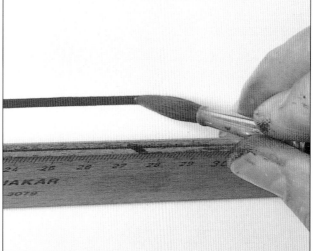

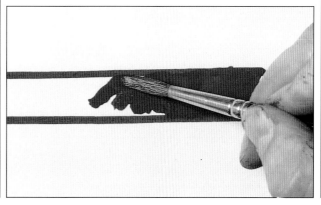

Chapter 5
Landscapes

Landscapes are perhaps one of the most traditional painting subjects and, for the beginner, can be one of the simplest and most accessible. As you will see from the two projects in this chapter, a landscape can be easy to produce yet, at the same time, the result can be a painting of depth and beauty. In the first project we concentrate on creating a simple scene, making full use of gouache's opacity. Whereas in the second we modestly mix media, starting with a rough base in acrylics upon which the gouache is applied. Both are very different approaches, but both produce wonderful finished paintings.

Although you can trace the roots of landscape painting back through history to Ancient Greece, incredibly it did not emerge as an art form in its own right until the past few hundred years. All through the Middle Ages the Christian Church, the greatest patron of the arts, commissioned paintings of a religious nature. Although artists painted landscapes in the backgrounds of their religious studies, it was only after the waning of the powers of the Church that a more natural realism was allowed to break through.

Nowadays our 'natural' environment tends to be man-made, consisting of concrete, brick and tarmac. However for this chapter we have decided to concentrate on the traditional style of the natural landscape. We cover the man-made variety in the next chapter.

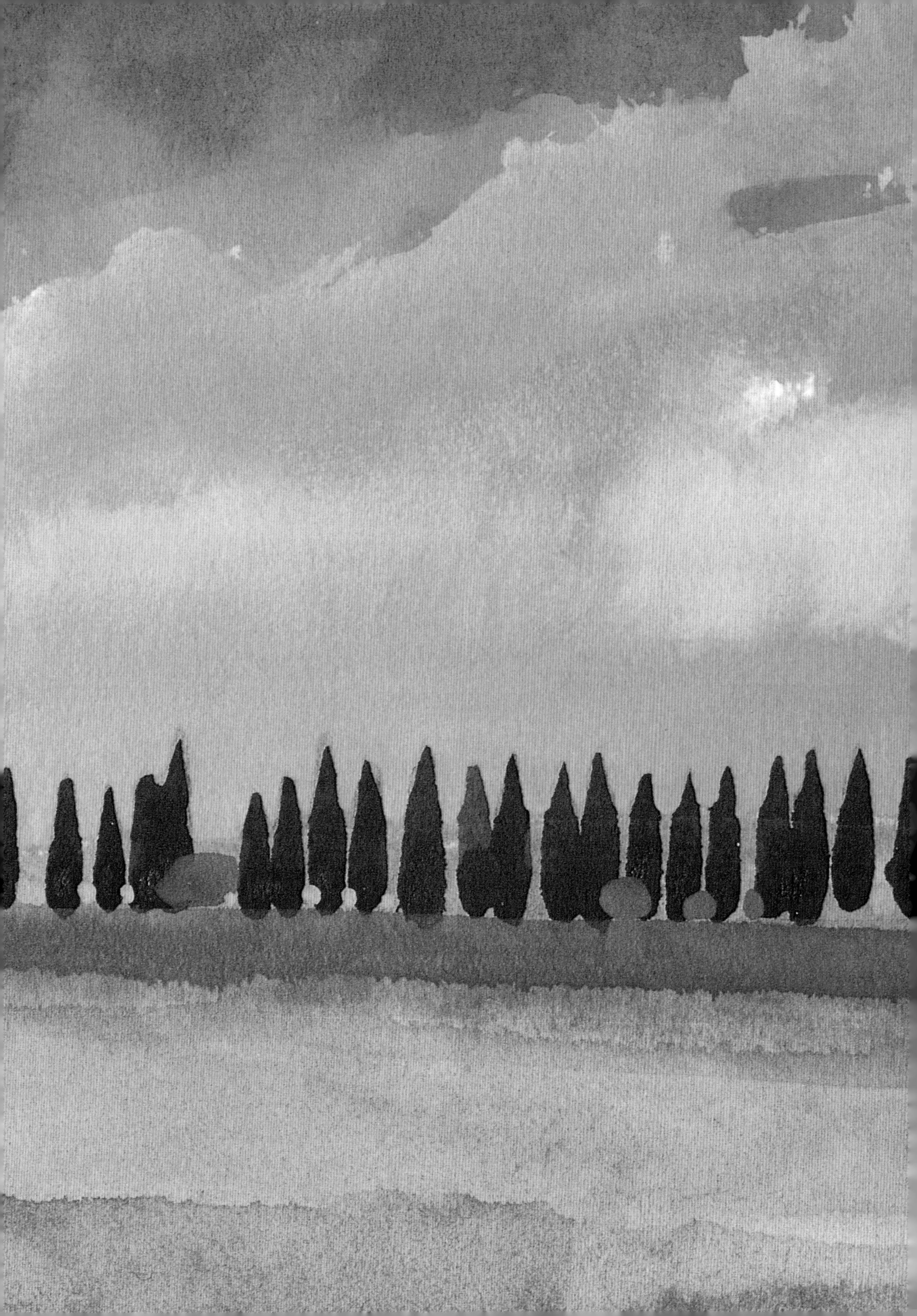

Yorkshire Dales

LANDSCAPES

Whilst walking on the Yorkshire Dales in the early autumn, it struck the artist that this scene would translate well into a painting. As he never goes anywhere unless armed with a camera, he was able to take a photograph and, once at home, file it in his own reference library. There is a lesson to be learnt here, and that is never leave home without a camera or sketch book as scenes may often present themselves when you are least expecting them. This approach enables you to build up your own library of pictures for further reference, so you will never run out of things to paint.

One of the major reasons for choosing this scene – apart from its natural beauty – is the harmony of the colours which makes it an ideal exercise for showing you how to work with a limited palette. This in turn allows you more time to concentrate on the form as you do not have to spend ages deciding which colour to use next. The ideal way to start is to choose around five or six colours. Here we have chosen forest green, Prussian blue, lemon yellow, yellow ochre and burnt umber. Before you begin, squeeze a small amount of each on to your palette and with a little water mix one into another and brush it onto a scrap of watercolour paper. Next bring in another colour and repeat the process. By the time you have finished you will be amazed by the number of colours you have created. It is also a good idea to note down next to each one what the mix is, because that way you can refer back to it and know exactly how to achieve a specific colour or tone. This may all sound very laborious, but it is an excellent way of familiarizing yourself with colours and will definitely pay off in the end.

1 As with most paintings, it is a good idea to make an initial pencil sketch. This allows you to map out the composition and make sure that all the elements of your picture are in the right place. Do not spend too much time on this as it is purely a rough guide that, at the end of the day, must not show through your finished painting. With a 2B pencil, make a loose sketch from the original reference photograph.

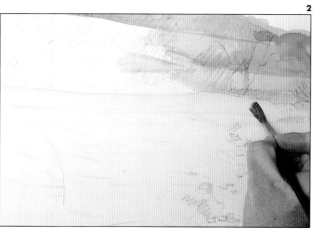

2 For this first stage of the painting you are going to start by laying an initial wash. With a mix of forest green, Prussian blue and lots of water, begin to lay in the hills at the top of the picture using a no. 6 sable brush. When this area is complete, add some lemon yellow to the mix and add in the areas of grass in the distance. Continue to work down the painting, adding more lemon yellow and a little forest green to vary the mix, but no more Prussian blue.

3 Once you have worked over the whole area add some yellow ochre to your previous mix and paint over the main area of grass again. To create a variation in the colour as you paint, keep adding in a little more yellow ochre for a darker tone or more water to lighten it. When you are happy with the end result, take some neat Prussian blue mixed with a lot of water and paint in the sky at the top right of the picture and the stream.

4 Add the Prussian blue wash to your main mix and now incorporate some burnt umber. Following your initial pencil sketch, paint in the trees and the dark areas of grass, again varying the tone to match your original reference. Once the trees have been established, add some more burnt umber and start to add the dark shadows of the rocks by the stream.

5 Continue to work on the shadows, gradually building them up as you go. When you have completed the shadows, and using the same mix of paint, move on to the grass and dry brush over the area to add the dark tufts, always referring back to your original reference. As you continue to work up the painting note how the colours are much more opaque. This is because the mix is relying on more pigment and less water. Work over the trees to add a little more definition and, with Prussian blue, forest green and a little water, darken the hills in the background.

6 You have now reached the stage in your painting when all the main elements have been established and it is time to switch to the detailed work. Before doing this, it is always sensible to take a step back and view your painting as a whole – this will enable you to decide whether any of the elements need further work. Switching to a no. 3 sable brush and a mix of Prussian blue and burnt umber, carefully paint in the main tree and bush to the right of the stream following your original sketch which should still just show through the layers of paint. When painting in details always hold the brush close to the head, which will give you maximum control. With the same mix add in the trunks and branches of the trees and then dry brush the copse on the right.

7 Switching back to your no. 6 sable brush, add some yellow ochre to the previous mix to liven it up. Returning to the grass, scumble over the area to add the warm tones that run through it and stretch down to the water's edge. With a new mix of forest green,

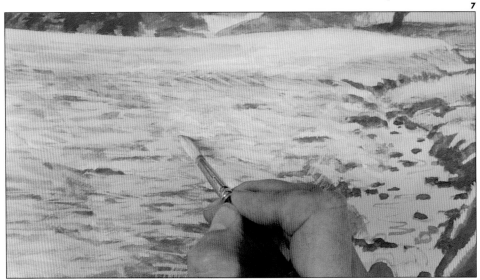

lemon yellow and white with a tiny amount of water, sharpen the line of grass directly below the trees. Using this same opaque mix (no added water), continue down the grass to the foreground picking out the texture. Add a little more white and lemon yellow, and use it to pick out the bright green highlights in the grass and amongst the rocks.

8 Now that you have finished the main area of the painting – the grass – you can start to think about the finishing touches. With a new mix of burnt umber and a little yellow ochre begin to add the brown highlights to the trees where the leaves have started to change into their autumn shades. Remember that with all these final stages hardly any water is used.

9 Returning to the mix of paint used at the end of step 7, add some yellow ochre and dry brush over the leaves of the trees to create the illusion of foliage. The next detail is to add the leaves to the bushes in front of the trees. When referring back to the original reference you can see two tiny highlights in the trees, so mix up a small amount of lemon yellow, forest green and white and dot them in. Use small specks of pure white to bring out the highlights in the stream where the sun hits the water. Now brush some patches of white down the length of the stream which will create the illusion of flowing water.

10 The painting is complete, so all you have to do now is stand back and admire your work. Note how the whole image has an overall feeling of harmony, which has been created through working with a limited palette of colours. But one of the most striking points about this painting is the vibrancy of the colours, which shows the true nature of gouache. Even though the starting point of this project was to lay a wash, once this had been established the artist immediately went on to exploit the opacity of gouache to its full potential. Several techniques such as dry brushing and scumbling were also used, but most importantly this painting shows how successful gouache is when painted light over dark. Without this capability, you would have had difficulty achieving the vibrancy of the shimmering sunlight on the grass and water.

9
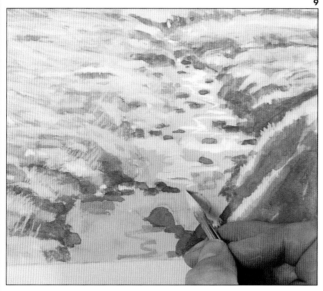

10

Sunflowers

LANDSCAPES

In the previous project we stressed the importance of never leaving home without your camera. However, in this case the reference came from a very different source – let it be another reminder for you to always keep your eyes open. The artist was on holiday in Tuscany, Italy, when he came across this selection of postcards depicting beautiful scenes of the surrounding countryside. The postcards are not only of an unusually high standard, but they also show the scenes at various times of the day. This type of reference supplies you with completely different skies, lighting and moods, without you having to hang around all day waiting for the sky to change.

This project is especially interesting because it makes use of a vibrant underpainting in acrylic paint. These brilliant colours set the scene early on, with the added advantage that acrylics, once dry, are not water-soluble and therefore will not dissolve when the gouache is applied. The project is also different because it is composed from several different postcards. Rather than simply painting the view shown on one of the postcards, the artist decided that he would amalgamate various elements from several to create the 'perfect' scene. The particularly dramatic sky and row of trees came from one shot, onto which the sunflowers from the other postcards were added.

1 For once you are not going to start by making an initial pencil sketch. Instead you use dilute liquid acrylic paint to launch straight into the underpainting. Using a no. 12 brush and some dilute ultramarine acrylic paint, roughly block in the area of sky. If you are working with a type of liquid acrylic, it can be used straight from the pot. Tube paint will need to be diluted a little with water. To this add some sap green and paint in the horizon line. Although the paint is running, do not worry as this will add to the effect of the painting. Now mix some process yellow and a tiny amount of marigold and lay in the area of fields in the foreground, going over the runs from the green mix.

2 Once the underpainting has dried, which will not be long as acrylics dry quickly, you can start to build up the picture in gouache. Starting with the horizon line, mix some permanent white, cobalt blue, yellow ochre and olive green with a little water and paint in the distant hills with a no. 8 brush. To this mix add some more olive green, a little extra cobalt blue and a small amount of ivory black to darken it, and carefully paint in the row of trees that runs along the horizon line.

3

3 The sky is next and this will need to be built up gradually to achieve the right sense of drama. Switching to a no. 11 brush, mix Prussian blue, a little olive green and permanent white with some water and start to paint in the darkest part of the sky at the top. With a fresh mix of cobalt blue, white and a little water, paint in the lower areas of the sky using very loose, almost random brush strokes. Note how the artist is holding the brush very close to the end, which also helps to achieve this loose way of working.

4 Whilst working on this part of the sky, do not get so carried away with this loose style that you end up painting over the trees. Leave them and their surrounding area alone until you are happy with the rest of the sky. When you are satisfied, switch to a no. 1 brush and with the same light sky mix of cobalt blue and white, carefully cut in around the trees to complete this area of the sky.

4

5 As we have already mentioned, the sky will need to be built up gradually. So, returning to the dark mix of Prussian blue, olive green and white, and switching back to your no. 11 brush, paint over the dark sky again with hardly any water in the mix. Repeat this for the lighter part of the sky with the cobalt blue and permanent white mix. Next you are going to create the clouds in a rather unusual way. Whilst the sky is still wet, load a no. 8 brush with some permanent white and literally roll it over the sticky paint.

6 Return to the tree mix of olive green, cobalt blue and a little ivory black, and paint in a few small extra trees on the horizon. Mix in a little more water and extend the green horizon line further down into the field. Now you can begin to work on the sunflowers. Add a little ivory black to some burnt sienna and, with a touch of water, start to paint in the seed clusters which form the centres of the flowers.

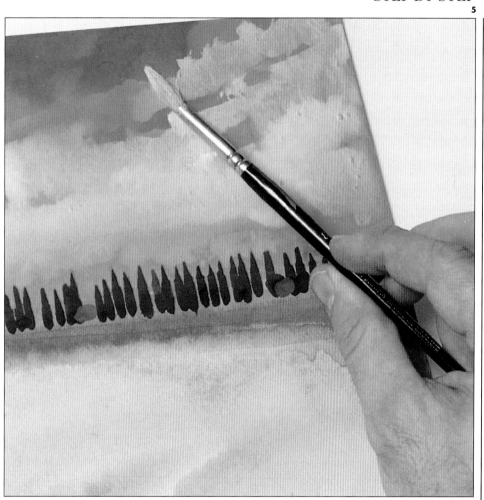

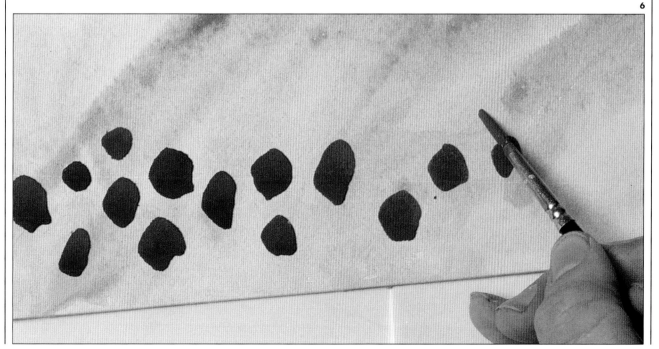

7

7   Add some olive green and more water to your seed mix, and, with the same no. 8 brush, start to lay a wash over the area of the fields where there are no sunflowers. As you do this make sure that you do not cut in tightly around the farthest row of seed heads –

instead leave a small surrounding area of yellow. The easiest way to do this – as it is rather fiddly – is to turn the painting on its side and pull the brush towards you. This will also avoid any possibility of runs from the wash ruining your sunflowers.

8   At this stage you are probably taking a deep breath and preparing yourself for the finely detailed – and time-consuming – task of painting in all the sunflowers, even though they become one mass of colour as they stretch towards the horizon. Well

relax, you are going to complete the sunflowers by using a very quick method. With the field mix of burnt sienna, ivory black and olive green but hardly any water, start to cut in around the seed heads in the foreground where the field shows through.

8

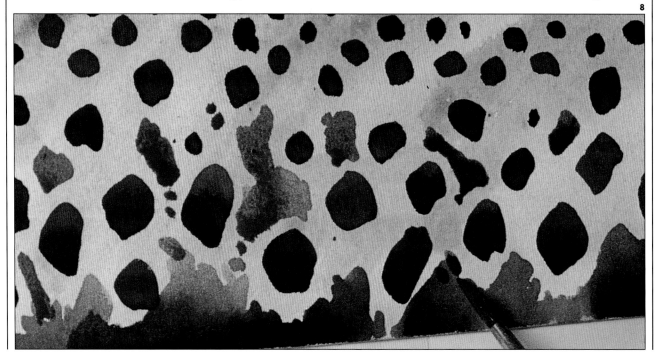

9 As you can see the process of painting in the negative shapes completes the sunflowers extremely quickly, and the style it creates fits in perfectly with the loose feel of the painting as a whole. Now there is only one more thing to do before you have finished. Turn the painting on its side once again and, with the previous mix, darken and define the line where the sunflowers end, which will really make them stand out.

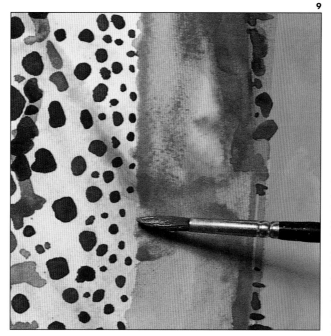

10 We hope that you have had fun painting this project in this loose style. The subject was perfect as it could be broken down into three bands – the sky, the horizon and the field – exactly as the artist did with his initial underpainting. Even though there is no such scene in Tuscany, it really does not matter. Hopefully this will encourage you to be more creative and to use your imagination when searching for the next scene to paint. This project is also quick to paint, which just goes to prove that not all paintings have to be painstakingly slow and meticulous to produce an acceptable and extremely pleasing end result.

Chapter 6
Man-made Environments

As we mentioned at the start of the previous chapter, today our 'natural' environment tends to be largely man-made. Therefore, in an attempt to show how art does not necessarily have to revolve around traditional approaches to traditional themes, in this chapter we concentrate on contemporary views of man-made environments.

The first project is of some fishing boats tied to a quayside. Although the subject matter is evidently man-made, it still has a traditional feel due to the associations with old fishing communities. Therefore this first project lies at a sort of half-way mark between the old and the new, and this is further emphasized by the viewpoint and the painting techniques employed.

The subject matter of the second project – some 200-year-old buildings – would also seem to indicate a half-way mark. However in this case the viewpoint showing only the rooftops gives the subject matter a contemporary flavour. In addition, great play is made of gouache's opaque quality which gives the painting an unexpected chalky texture.

In the course of these projects you will be introduced to painting various man-made materials, including brick, concrete, slate and metal. With this experience we hope that you will feel able to tackle virtually any man-made environment presented to you, be it an old shepherd's hut or the Empire State Building.

French Fishing Boats

MAN-MADE ENVIRONMENTS

This composition was chosen not only because boats are always fun to paint, but also because this particular viewpoint presents you with an unexpected perspective on a traditional scene. It was taken whilst our artist was strolling along the quayside of a little harbour in France.

This project is mainly an exercise in working from light to dark by gradually increasing the amount of pigment, which is very similar to painting in pure watercolour. Even though the opacity of gouache is reduced when diluted, you will find that it does not handle in the same way as pure watercolour and the result will be less translucent. However, for this project, the main advantage of gouache is the intensity of the colours, as is so evident over the following pages.

1

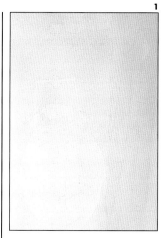

2

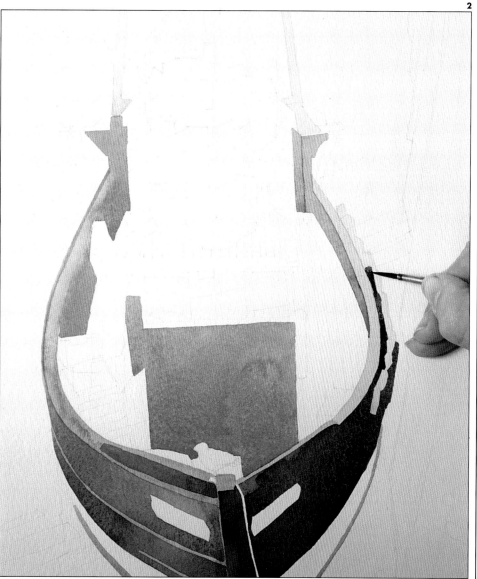

1 For this painting it is particularly important to make a precise pencil drawing first, especially of the boat as it contains quite a bit of detail. Do this with a 2B pencil but do not press too hard because the lines need to be fairly light to avoid them showing through in the finished painting. With a no. 5 sable brush and a very watery mix of cobalt blue and cadmium yellow, lay a wash over the area of sea, carefully following the contours of the boats. Switching to a no. 12 sable brush and another very watery mix of cobalt blue and ivory black, lay a wash over the posts along the sea wall.

3

2 Change to a no. 4 sable brush and with a mix of cobalt blue and ivory black with lots of water, locate the blue areas on the boat and also the small boat in the background. Start by painting the framework of the winch that supports the nets, moving down to the lightest shades. As you can see, there are tonal variations in the blue. To achieve this, keep to the same mix, but for the darker areas use the paint neat adding no extra water and, for the very darkest areas, raise the ratio of ivory black.

3 Staying with the boat, take some red ochre and mix it with yellow ochre – to make a rusty, brownish red colour – and using it fairly neat, paint in the red areas. Again not forgetting the boats in the background, add more water to the mix to make it lighter, and paint in their red areas. Once the red has dried, paint in the light highlight that runs down the life belt to the right of the cabin on the main boat and the rope fenders on the small boats with some orange lake light.

4

5

6

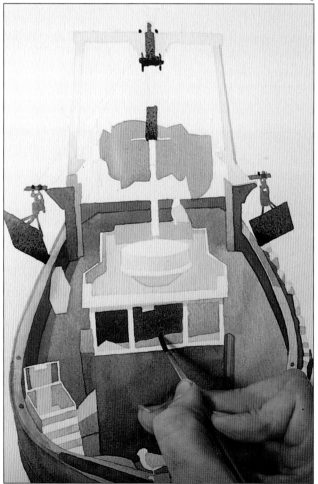

4 With a fairly watery mix of raw umber and ivory black, block in the deck of the main boat. Add a little more water and paint in the hulls – on the right only – of the boats in the background. Switching to a grey mix of indigo with a little ivory black and plenty of water, block in all the windows on the boats, as well as the top of the cabin and the fish box on the main boat.

5 Returning to the grey window mix, add in more indigo and a little ivory black, but no water, and paint in the dark reflections on the windows of all the boats, the fish boxes of the main boat and the wings of the seagull. These need to be crisp so the paint

must be applied wet-on-dry. Now take some olive green mixed with lots of water and paint in the net of the main boat, as well as the boat in the background.

6 Continuing to work on the details, return to your grey wash of indigo and ivory black – with the same emphasis on the indigo and no more water – to paint in the shackles and the metal plates which guide the nets through the water. Once these elements are complete overpaint the reflections of the windows on the main boat only, and the numbers on the plate, using the same mix.

7 At this stage it is a good idea to take a break while the painting dries, before returning to take an overall view of the painting to check that you are happy with the way that it is progressing. If you are in a hurry, a hairdryer is very useful to speed the drying time up, but be careful to keep it on a low heat and not too close to the painting, otherwise the paint gets pushed around, and you could end up with unwanted dark areas where the paint collects. With a watery mix of ivory black and a little indigo, add the darker shadow on the net. Then switch to a no. 8 sable brush and lay a wash over the posts along the sea wall and the top.

8

9

8 Switching back to a no. 4 sable brush, mix a little yellow ochre into some venetian red with lots of water and lay a base wash over the areas of brickwork. The final wash for the sea wall consists of a watery mix of olive green and a touch of alazarin crimson. This is for the bottom portion of the sea wall where the water rises and forms a thick layer of algae.

9 Now that the base washes have been laid on the sea wall, it is just a matter of building up the areas of darker tones. So, returning to the mix of ivory black and indigo, add a little more of each colour as well as a little raw umber to darken it even further and paint a second coat over the posts, remembering not to add any more water. If you want the edges to be crisp, as in this case, you must make sure that the original washes are completely dry before you do any overpainting. Repeat this for the areas of algae by adding more olive green to the original wash. Finally, using a fresh mix of orange lake light, brown madder alizarin and a little ivory black with a drop of water, paint in broken bands of colour to create the effect of brickwork.

10   As all the main elements of the painting are completed, the sea, in contrast, is looking extremely neglected. Returning to your original sea wash of cobalt blue and cadmium yellow, darken it by adding more paint but no extra water as it was very watery to begin with. Start by loosely painting the wide bands of shadows across the sea, varying the tone with the addition of more paint for the darker areas around the front of the boats where they are reflected in the water.

11   To complete the sea area you will need a fresh mix of olive green, indigo and a little ivory black with some added water. With this mix, start to paint in the really dark reflections on the water around the main boat and the boats in the background. Wait for this to dry, then darken the mix by adding more paint and over-paint all of these areas again.

12   The final stage of this painting is adding all the intricate details of the wires to the winch. With some ivory black and hardly any water, start to paint in the rigging and add the two dark blocks on either side of the top of the cabin. To do this you need a very steady hand so that you create a fluid line which is not too ponderous or thick. It might be a good idea to practise on some spare paper first. Try not to grasp the brush too tightly or the line will lose its spontaneity. At this point, the artist took a good look at the painting and decided that the sea needed extra work. So he returned to the original mix of cobalt blue and cadmium yellow and added in some extra ripples around the main boat.

13 Now you can
return to the ivory
black mix and finish
off the details of the
winch and the aerials
on all of the boats.
This should be the
very final stage, but
on taking a final
overall view of the
painting and
comparing it to the
original reference, the
posts along the sea
wall look far too flat
and lack the texture
of old weather-beaten
wood. The thought of
painting in all those
lines running down
them was far too
daunting, so here is a
little trick: Once the
painting is totally
dry, take a graphite
pencil and just draw
them in! As you can
see, this creates the
desired effect, but in
a fraction of the time.

Rooftops

MAN-MADE ENVIRONMENTS

The interest in this rooftop view has been provided by the architecture – especially the abundant chimney pots – and through the unusual perspective. The artist recently moved to the town of Bath, and this scene is a view from one of his windows looking down a steep hill – hence the high viewpoint of what are actually four-storey buildings. The viewpoint is roughly in the centre of the picture since you can see the top of the mansard roof on the left, but not the ones on the right. In addition, the perspective is further complicated by the fact that the buildings are around two hundred years old and have experienced quite a bit of subsidence through the years.

The artist took a few shots of this scene and brought them with him when it came time to make this book. Unfortunately they were on 35mm slides. Although it is possible to work from a slide, it is easier to take it down to your local photocopying shop and get a colour laser-copy run out. This service is now widely available and is remarkably cheap considering the quality and size of the print you get. The original shot included more buildings and extended down to the pavement, so the artist cut out a small rectangular 'window' from a piece of card and placed it in various places over the print until he arrived at the view shown below.

Since there is very little variation in colour – mostly tinted shades of grey – it was decided that an exceptionally limited palette would be used to create one basic mix that would suffice for virtually the whole painting. This exercise will therefore be a real test of your mixing skills, since the various tones are created by shifting the emphasis in the mix from one colour to another or by lightening and darkening it.

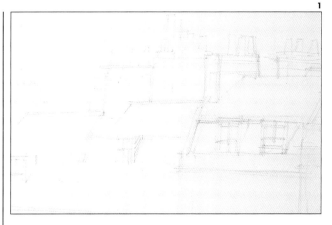

1 As with most gouache projects the starting place is to make an outline sketch with a soft pencil, such as a 2B, on a piece of pre-stretched paper (see page 42). Do not spray fixative over these marks since they will be allowed to blend and merge into the painting so that they gradually fade away.

2 Use a no. 6 Series 7 brush to lay a broad band of very dilute Prussian blue across the top third of the painting. Then continue immediately by covering the middle third with a wash of dilute yellow ochre, and the remainder with dilute cadmium orange. If you do this quickly enough the colours will run together on the paper, so

creating a gentle gradation of tone from top to bottom.

3 Before the washes have had a chance to completely dry, dab over them with a wad of tissue to remove any excess

paint and to create some interesting texture. You will not be conscious of this texturing in your finished work but it will certainly contribute to the subtle depths achieved in the painting.

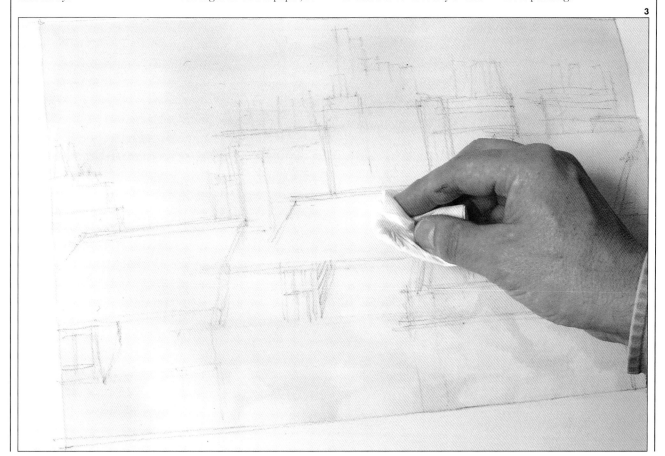

4 The form of the buildings will be built up in several layers of different coloured wet-in-wet washes, each covering various portions of the painting to create a wide variety of tone. Start with a mixture of black and cadmium red for a browny/red tone over the roof of the central building.

5 Before this has had a chance to dry, create a watery mix of Prussian blue, black and cadmium red and lay a thin wash wet-in-wet from the tops of the chimneys down to the base of the painting. Vary the mix as you go so that some areas will lean towards red, while others have a blue bias.

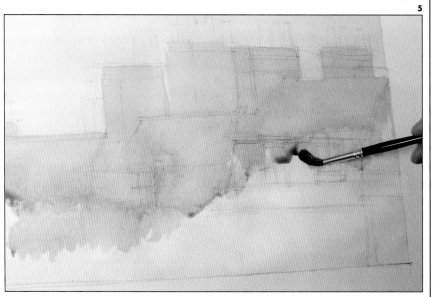

4

5

6

6 For the next wash mix together Prussian blue and small amounts of cadmium red and cadmium orange. The combination of the red and orange will make the Prussian blue appear slightly grey (a slate grey for the roof tiles), but will not be as harsh as the black you added in the previous step. Lay this as a wash from the chimney stacks (leaving the pots as they were) down to the base of the picture, but making sure that you do not paint over the shapes of the windows. If you paint the washes in quick succession the colours will merge on the paper and so create further tonal variations for you.

7 Continuing with the same mix of Prussian blue, cadmium red and cadmium orange – but this time with less water so it will appear darker – overpaint the dark side of the chimney stacks and the sloping roofs of the two buildings to the right. You can now allow the painting to dry fully before proceeding any further. Once it is dry you will notice that you have already suggested quite a lot of form to the buildings simply by laying down these rather undefined washes.

8 Still using the same mixture, lay a wash down the front of the building to the right. Apply the colour in horizontal bands, starting at the top with a heavy emphasis towards the Prussian blue and then gradually increasing the amount of cadmium red and cadmium orange towards the bottom to indicate the weathering on the building's surface. The fragment of building frontage visible on the far right can then be blocked in with your original blue/grey mixture.

Allow the washes to dry and then darken your mix by diluting it less. Use this to paint a dark band across the front of each building where the guttering falls.

9

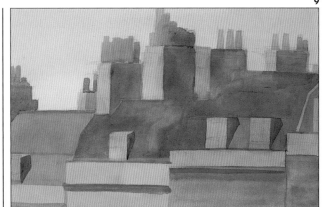

9 With the same dark version of the mix, carefully block in the sides of the dormer windows. Then dilute it with some more water and lay another wash over all the roofs and the dark side of the chimney stacks.

Next concentrate on the chimney pots themselves, which until this point have received very little attention. The same colours are used, but the emphasis is shifted to create three distinct tones – blue, grey and terracotta. The blue tone leans towards more Prussian blue in the mix, the grey is much more of an equal blend of the constituent colours, whilst the terracotta tone is created by adding in lots more cadmium orange.

10

10 Now you can begin to work up the form of the dormer windows. Initially use a dark grey mixture of Prussian blue, cadmium red and cadmium orange – but this time with a small amount of cadmium yellow added to make it slightly green – to lay a dark, almost black, background colour that will be distinct from the colour of the mansard roofs.

11

11 Once the first layer of paint on the windows has dried, use the same tone to overpaint the shadowy areas in each window, but this time with much less water in the mix so that it appears darker. You can also use this tone to paint the shaded side of the ridges running down between the roofs and, with more water, the windows on the front of the building to the right.

12

12 Finally, with your very dark green/grey mix, paint in the shadows cast by the chimney stacks and include the guttering running along the front of the buildings. Then return to your original blue/grey mix (which had no added yellow) and use it to overpaint the sloping portions of the roofs to differentiate them from the near vertical sections at the front.

Whilst you have been painting these bits and pieces the windows should have had a chance to dry, so you can now add detailing over the top. Mix permanent white with a touch of yellow ochre to warm it up, but do not include any water so that it remains totally opaque. Then, again using the no. 3 Series 7 brush, delicately pick out the window frames.

13

13 With the same mix of permanent white and yellow ochre, paint the thin highlighted areas on the front of the buildings to the right. Then add in a small amount of Prussian blue to turn the mixture into a light grey and paint the highlights running along the guttering, the very thin strip at the top of the front wall, and the frames around the two windows on the front of the same building. Allow the painting to dry so that you can work these windows up further.

14 You can now paint the curtains visible through the two windows. Return to your original grey mix of Prussian blue, cadmium red and cadmium orange and put in a couple of thin bands running down each window. Add permanent white and yellow ochre into the mix, and fill in the gaps between the bands. Finally, increase the amount of Prussian blue so that you can include the shadows on the left of each window.

A very dark version of your grey mix can then be used to express the ridges on the chimney stacks to finish them off.

15 Turning your attention to the chimney pots, you will find that, in comparison with the rest of the painting which has been worked up, they will by now look rather pale and insignificant. So use the same three colours – Prussian blue, cadmium red and cadmium orange – to repaint them a darker tone and, as in step 9, shift the emphasis to create different tones for the various types of pot. Once the pots have been sufficiently darkened down, add some permanent white to the mixture for some soft highlights.

16 The final step is to suggest the roof tiles. Dilute your grey mix so that it will not appear too harsh, and paint in horizontal lines along the roofs. Then go back and add in vertical lines to complete the tiles. You could run the brush along a ruler to get a perfect straight line, but your painting will look more realistic if you paint them freehand. Any breaks or variations in your lines will only contribute to the impression that these tiles are in fact old and therefore unlikely to be in highly regimented rows.

17 At last you can step back and view your finished work. Even at this stage you may notice a part of the painting that needs further attention, but be careful not to overdo this as you could easily overwork your painting and spoil it.

As promised in the introduction to this project, one mix of three colours was used for virtually the whole painting, producing some impressive variations in tone and hue. Limiting your palette in such a way can be helpful in expressing the interesting forms of the architecture and the shadows cast by it. In fact, as with this project, paintings of buildings are often restricted to coloured greys, be it representing concrete, stone or slate. This lack of obvious colour may make painting buildings seem rather an unattractive prospect, but in fact this frees you to concentrate on capturing form and mastering the rules of perspective as explained in chapter 2. And, quite simply, there are some beautiful buildings out there just waiting to be painted!

Chapter 7
Abstract

If you look up the word 'abstract' in a dictionary it will probably say something along the lines of 'idealistic', 'not practical' or 'free from representational qualities' – all of which are rather abstract statements in themselves! What abstract art is truly about is using form, colour and texture for their own aesthetic ends, with no conscious attempt to represent recognizable objects.

People often reject the notion of abstract art out-of-hand. In fact what they are normally referring to is abstract expressionism. This was developed in New York in the 1940s as a means of illustrating spontaneous expression through abstract forms. The movement produced 'action' painting, an art form made famous by Jackson Pollock who threw the paint at his canvas and allowed it to drip down. Many find such work difficult to appreciate but you can always turn to another, more aesthetic, branch of abstract art.

In this chapter we shy away from 'action' painting – there would only be one step, throwing the paint! – instead we present you with two contrasting abstract works. The first is a simple landscape which is refined and abstracted in terms of form, colour and texture. This project is the perfect introduction for the beginner and leads logically on to the second set piece. Here we drop all links with the world as we know it and go for a journey into the artist's brain. We hope you enjoy the trip.

Egyptian Village

ABSTRACT

For this introduction to the world of abstract painting we decided to ease you in gently with a purely graphic interpretation of a real scene. The picture is broken down into large areas of flat colour, reducing the tones to a minimum. The vibrancy of the colours used adds greatly to the success of the image, pushing what is already a rather unusual scene into the world of the semi-surreal.

The reference photograph was taken by the artist from a moving coach (hence the quality) whilst he was on holiday in Egypt, passing through a village called Qurnah just outside Luxor. As you can see from the finished painting on page 91, the scene was refined to its basics and any elements of clutter were dropped. Then the basic shapes were reduced to solid blocks of colour, ignoring areas of changing tone.

This abstraction of a scene is probably the simplest form of abstract painting for the novice to get to grips with. Solid panels of primary colour with no obvious order or form – as made famous by Mondrian – may appear to be an easy route to follow, but getting others to appreciate your work may prove difficult. Painting what you imagine

and feel – as with the project on page 92 – is great fun, but it can take some time to really let yourself go. Instead this project falls into a middle ground, not only between the different types of abstract work but also between the world of abstract and more traditional painting. By abstracting a real scene, the project is made easier since it still conforms to a recognizable scene, yet you are breaking away from reality into the realms of imagination.

STEP BY STEP

1 Having stretched your paper the day before, start by using an HB pencil to make a fairly detailed outline drawing, reducing the scene before you to basic shapes. Since these exploratory lines could show through in your finished painting, it is important to make sure you are happy with the initial drawing. So take your time, and erase any unwanted or incorrectly placed marks. Your first mix is of permanent white, yellow ochre and a touch of ivory black, and you use this to lay a thin wash over the background hills and the foreground sand with a no. 12 sable brush.

2 Once your first wash is dry, you can paint another thin, watery coat of the same colour over those areas destined to be darker. Allow this second layer of paint to dry fully before continuing.

Now turn your mixture into more of a grey/brown colour by increasing the percentage of black and by including a little bit of ultramarine, then use this to paint a flat wash over all the mud walls. This is a base colour which will become the light tone showing through the bricks yet to be painted. Support your painting at a slight tilt so that these washes dry darker towards the bottom to create the effect of shadows.

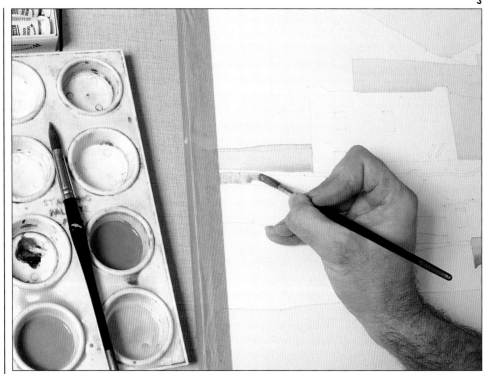

3 Next create a blue/grey tone by mixing together permanent white, ultramarine and ivory black, and use this to paint the blue wall on the left of the painting and the step at the foot of the door. Since these are quite small areas, you will find it easier with a finer brush such as a no. 8 sable. Add more white and water to lighten the mixture for the small block in the centre of the painting. With these areas dry, paint in the building between them with a very weak wash of the same colour. The colours must not run together so each area has to be totally dry before you continue to paint.

4 Mix together yellow ochre and brilliant yellow ochre to create a very strong and vivid yellow, and use this colour to block in the wall on the left and the two yellow buildings. Brilliant yellow ochre on its own tends to be a bit harsh, but it is easy to tone it down with standard yellow ochre. You will find that toning down such powerful colours with blues or blacks will tend to deaden them a bit too much.

5

6

5 Again, allow the entire painting to dry and then combine turquoise blue with a little ultramarine (to take the edge off) for the building on the far right. If you want to speed up the drying process you can always use a hairdryer on a low heat, holding it far enough away from the picture surface to ensure that the colour is not pushed around the paper.

6 Next, make your turquoise and ultramarine mixture more blue by adding more ultramarine, and then use it to paint the shutters, not forgetting the one on the blue building you have just blocked in. Then turn this into a blue/grey tone by adding titanium white and ivory black for the shadow running along under the roof of the building in the centre.

7 You can now complete three sections of the painting in quick succession – the brown door·and windows, the green shutters in the centre and the red base of the building to its left. Create the brown colour by adding black to yellow ochre and, with a no. 2 sable brush, paint the three windows and the main door at the front. This mix can also be used to paint the zig-zag effect on the yellow building to the right. Since yellow ochre is the base for this colour it harmonizes with the bright yellow used previously. The green shutters in the centre are simply painted with straight permanent middle green, and you create the red tone for the bottom of the house by mixing cadmium red pale with a touch of ivory black to slightly deaden the colour.

7

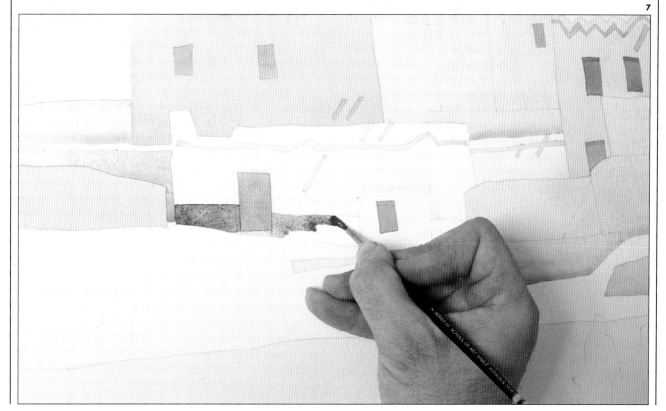

ABSTRACT / EGYPTIAN VILLAGE

8   You can now turn to the two hard shadows cast on the buildings to the right. Both are darker versions of the original base colour for the buildings – yellow ochre and brilliant yellow ochre for the yellow building and turquoise blue and ultramarine for the blue one – with black being added into the mix to darken the tone down.

9   To complete the buildings you only need to fill in the brickwork mentioned earlier. Re-create your original mud colour – permanent white, yellow ochre, ivory black and a little bit of ultramarine – but make it slightly darker by increasing the percentage of black and ultramarine. With your no. 2 sable brush, paint broken bands of colour across the original mud wall areas to create the effect of rough bricks. It is probably a good idea to practise this technique on a scrap of paper before applying it to the painting itself. Once all the brickwork has dried, darken the mix further by adding more black and use this to paint the very darkest areas at the top, the triangular shadows towards the foreground and the small window to the right.

10 Now darken some yellow ochre with ivory black to create dark brown and use this to add the shadow around the door frame. You also use the same colour to add in the feet and hands of the three figures in the foreground. Once this has dried, and continuing with your no. 2 sable brush, use straight ivory black to paint the main form of the figures. Finally, returning to your brick mixture from step 8, paint in the vague form of the shadows cast by the figures.

11 You can now step back and view your first finished abstract painting. Did you notice how you worked from light to dark as if you were using pure watercolour? Although the major advantage of gouache over its more well-known relative is the ability to paint light colours over dark ones, you do not necessarily always have to take this course. This painting could have been painted dark to light, but since the scene was fairly light anyway it lent itself more to the 'light to dark' approach, with extensive use of very pale washes. It is important to remember that just because you are using gouache you do not need to feel constrained to work in one particular way. If another method suits the scene better, then by all means make use of it. What really makes this painting stand out from one done in pure watercolour is the greater vividness of the colours due to the opacity of gouache. This scene was abstracted by a number of methods, but one of the most important is the vivid use of flat colour, which would not have been as successful if painted with pure watercolour.

We are sure that you will have enjoyed this introduction to the world of abstract painting, but before you decide to paint hundreds of scenes in this manner, why not give the following project a go. It leads you deep into the realms of the truly abstract, with the artist letting his imagination take total control. From there it is just one small step to total insanity!

10

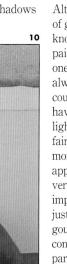

11

Scene from Another World

ABSTRACT

We decided not to base this abstract project upon anything recognizable or familiar. Although in the step-by-step instructions that follow we refer to the main shape as a screen – as, indeed, you could take it as a television or computer screen – this is merely for convenience. By referring to it as a screen, we are relating it to something familiar which in turn will create a link with the accepted world of reality. Trying to relate an abstract image to reality is often a mistake made when judging an abstract painting. It is easy to see why so many people react to the works of Mondrian, Picasso or any other abstract painter, along the lines of: 'I could do better myself.' The reason for these criticisms is that they are trying to find recognizable objects in the painting. Yet in an abstract painting, it is the interaction of shape and colour which can produce emotions and stimulate the intellect without necessarily making any reference to everyday objects.

The same pictorial devices and techniques used to paint a realistic scene may still be used to paint an abstract, as can the same methods of describing form and space. The artist uses the gouache here to produce an opaque, flat surface with hard edges. Obviously this project comes from the imagination of our particular artist and therefore will probably mean very little to you. Sometimes an abstract artist is trying to express thoughts and ideas, in other words trying to hold a conversation with the viewer, while at other times the painting is a stream of consciousness which need not involve an audience. We are asking you to produce the latter sort of abstract. However cynical you are, sit down and take some time on your own and let your imagination run wild. This should play an important part in any artist's life anyway, but for once take inspiration from inside yourself. You will be amazed how relaxing and freeing the whole experience can be. So, throw caution to the wind and paint whatever comes into your head. After all there is no need for embarrassment as you do not ever have to show it to anyone!

Here you can see the gradual progression of coloured pencil sketches that finally led to this step-by-step project. This is where a sketchbook really proves its worth, since the moment an idea enters your head, you can quickly jot it down and then work on it at your leisure.

1

1 The design produced by the artist may seem random but he manipulates the emotions of the viewer through the juxtaposition of colour, in particular, and through pattern. Once you are happy with your coloured pencil design, lay the initial outline drawing onto watercolour paper. Normally you would use a graphite pencil, but in this case use a coloured pencil which is much softer and will not matter if it shows through. Using a no. 6 Series 7 sable brush, mix some turquoise and permanent white with a small amount of water and start to block in the parallel bands in the foreground. The mix for the sides of the bands is ultramarine and permanent white, again with very little water. The reason for choosing these two colours is that the turquoise contains yellow and blue and ultramarine is a red - blue, therefore when they are placed next to each other the whole colour spectrum is expressed in the two blues.

2

2 Before starting this next stage, paint a second coat over the blues, aiming for a really smooth finish and avoiding any obvious brushstrokes. Now, mix some cadmium red, permanent green middle and permanent white with a little water and paint in the grey frame of the screen. For the stripes at the bottom, paint the darker red in pure cadmium red with a little water and the lighter stripes with a mix of cadmium orange and cadmium yellow, again with hardly any water. The central stripe is painted in alizarin rose madder mixed with a lot of permanent white. You can now paint the triangle by starting with cadmium red and grading it into cadmium orange. This can be done on the paper as you are using hardly any water, which in turn gives you more control over the paint. As with all these stages, they will need a second coat of paint for a super-smooth finish, but make sure it is not too thick or it will crack or flake.

3 The next step is to fill in the swirls of colour within the screen. The first shape above the stripes is spectrum violet mixed with a lot of permanent white and the next one is alizarin rose madder with a lot of white. Again, as with all these mixes, there is hardly any water. At the top of the screen the alternating colours are achieved with cadmium orange and cadmium yellow.

4 Having talked you through all the various colours of the main shapes, you can see that to complete this work all you need to do is fill in the screen. So, at this point, we suggest that you stand back and take a good overall look at the painting so far and decide for yourself what colours you personally would like to choose. After all this is not a painting of anything that exists, so it can be made up of any colours you wish.

5 Hopefully you have decided to make your own mark on this painting and choose your own colours or even shapes within the screen. After all, there is no real process or any guiding rules to this painting. The artist simply improvised and made decisions as he went. However, if you do want to recreate the crisp, straight edges of the grey frame, load your brush with a small amount of the original grey mix but with a little less white. Hold a ruler, tipped up on its side, and run the ferrel (the metal band) of your brush along it with the tip of the bristles touching the paper. The ruler will keep the brush steady, so giving you a perfectly straight line.

6 Although the original idea behind this image was of suspended objects, on further consideration the artist felt that there should be a background to pull and connect the shapes together and, in turn, that it should be fairly neutral so as not to intrude or detract from the main shapes. Mix some cadmium red pale, permanent green middle and lots of permanent white with very little water and fill in all the white background area.

Whatever your thoughts are on this painting, at least you cannot deny that it is a totally different way of working and in fact it is a very good exercise in the use of gouache with very little water. Because of the opacity of gouache and its consistency when used in this form it is possible to cover areas of flat colour with a completely even and smooth finish. Can you see any signs of a brushstroke anywhere on this painting?

5

6

Chapter 8
Animals

The subject of animals can be extremely challenging for the beginner and requires a lot of practise. However, once you get into the swing of things it becomes immensely rewarding.

The most obvious problem is that, unlike the human figure, you cannot ask an animal to pose for you. Tame animals are always on the move and wild animals normally bolt off in the other direction the moment they see a human coming. In fact you would be lucky even to see the animal let alone paint it!

The second main problem for the beginner is lack of experience in capturing such diverse textures as fur, feathers, scales, etc. On top of this, no art class would ever be able to teach you the anatomy of every type of animal you may want to paint. Your own preference could be anything from a hippopotamus to a gerbil, a dragonfly to an aardvark. The various coats can be covered – we concentrate on fur and feathers in this chapter – but when it comes to the anatomy lessons... forget it! What you must learn to do is to study your subject carefully. Natural history museums can be useful, but you will probably have more fun at a zoo or a safari park where the animals have a chance to move around. For your painting do lots of rough sketches first, before plotting it out in pencil. Take your time and only pick up a brush when you are totally happy that you have captured the form of the animal.

Leopard

ANIMALS

Everyone has their own particular favourite animal, but few could fail to be inspired by the proud and beautiful leopard. The only problem with painting such an exotic beast is finding a suitable model. Zoos can be some help, but you are then normally limited to painting a rather sad and bored caged animal which inevitably will not be at its best. The perfect solution would be to go on safari in Africa, but for most of us this is not an option. So the answer has to be photographic reference. This fine example was found in an old library book.

The advantage of photographic reference is not only that the subject will remain still, but that you have time to consider the composition and so alter and refine it in any way you feel fit. In this case, we decided to heighten the impact of the scene by placing just the adult leopard on a rocky crag in front of a rich sunset.

The real challenge when painting animals is to make sure that you capture their form correctly. Even with a leopard – which, to be honest, is not the sort of creature you encounter very often – if you make its body too long or its legs too short the viewer will instinctively know that your painting is wrong. So, take your time, and only start painting when you are satisfied that your initial drawing is perfect – use tracing paper or a scaled grid if necessary.

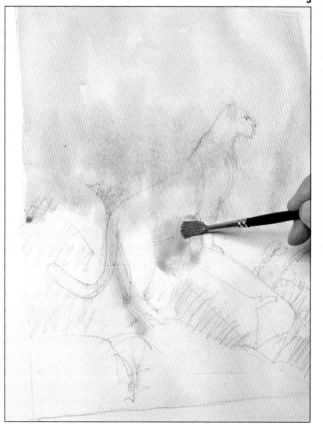

1   For this project select a rather rough surfaced paper which will better suit the texture of the main subject. Remember to stretch it the day before. You can buy ready stretched paper (as was used here), but you do pay for the privilege. Mark out your initial outline drawing with a 2B pencil. However, do not fix the pencil marks as they will be merge into the paint and so gradually disappear as the picture progresses.

2   Before you start mixing up your paints, use a large wash brush to wet the entire paper. This means that when you begin to lay down some colour, it will spread into the wash of water to create some interesting accidental textures that make a good starting point and may be utilized later on.

3   Start the painting by laying an initial all-over colour of yellow ochre and burnt sienna randomly applied with a no. 6 sable brush. Tilt the picture towards you, mixing the colours as you go. The colours will merge and spread because the paper is damp from the water you laid on it. Pick up any excess paint that collects at the bottom of the picture with the tip of a dry brush. The paper will probably buckle alarmingly because of the double wash. But do not worry as it will dry flat.

4   Before the painting has quite dried, continue by roughly painting in the darker area at the bottom with dilute burnt umber mixed with a small amount of black. Then, again, allow the painting to dry partially, before applying straight black with a no. 6 sable brush to further build up the form of the rocks. With this method of painting over the still-damp previous layer, you will get a small amount of blending taking place on the paper which will blur the edges and create further mixed colours. It does not matter too much at this stage if your painting appears rather loose, since you will tighten up the effect with subsequent layers of opaque paint.

5   Mix together yellow ochre, burnt sienna and burnt umber and block in the form of the leopard. This creates a basic middle tone for the cat's coat that will be worked up at a later stage. Add in some more burnt umber to the mix and continue painting down into the rocks to promote harmony in the colour of both the leopard and its background. In addition, this will also help build up the form of the rocks. You will return to

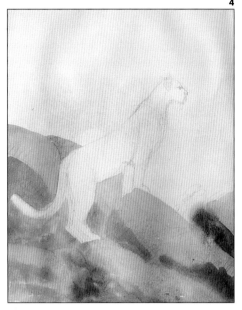

the rocks repeatedly with less and less dilute paint until they have been fully established, then you will switch to fully opaque paint to add the highlight areas over the top.

6   Once the painting has dried, use the same mix to repaint the darker areas of the leopard and then continue with the build-up of the rocks by re-painting the shadow areas. Now mix burnt umber into some permanent green middle and use it to block in the foliage. You can paint in a wider area of colour here than

is necessary since you will cut in around it with the background colour later to create the real shapes of the greenery. By putting down plenty of colour now, it gives you more scope to decide exactly how to paint the foliage when the time comes. To increase the range of tone in the green areas, apply a black wash around them before they are dry so that the two colours run together slightly.

7   Now, use black, warmed up with a dash of burnt umber, to paint over all the dark areas

in the rocks. Transfer this mix to the dark areas on the leopard – the snout, eyes and ears – and then add in more water for the slightly lighter areas – the mouth and the backs of the front legs. Whilst the painting dries, stand back and have a good look at what you have done so far. These breaks are very handy for assessing how the painting has gone so far and therefore deciding what you are going to do next. Obviously, in this case you do not have much of a choice as you are following a step-by-step!

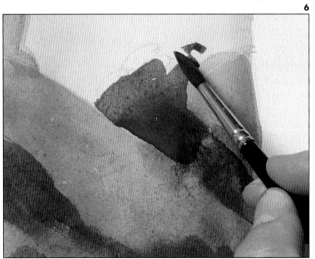

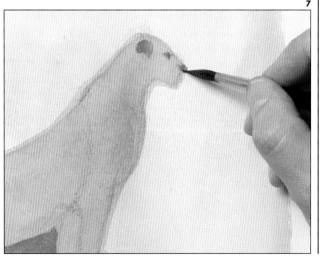

8 You can now introduce a new colour – alizarin rose madder. Since this subject is to be painted against a glorious sunset, it is important to introduce points of rosy reflected light in all the various elements, creating an overall harmony in the colours. Dilute the alizarin with plenty of water and then lay a wash over the entire leopard and all the rocks. Inevitably, the suggestion of foliage will be lost slightly when you lay the alizarin, so go back and re-paint the areas of green. From now on you will be working with opaque paint, so allow the painting to dry completely.

9 You have already done quite a bit of work to the rocks, so therefore this is the perfect place to start. Use permanent white mixed with a bit of ivory black, alizarin rose madder and burnt umber to start painting in the highlighted areas on the rocks. Constantly refer back to the reference photograph to make sure you do not paint too much of the rocks with this light tone.

8

9

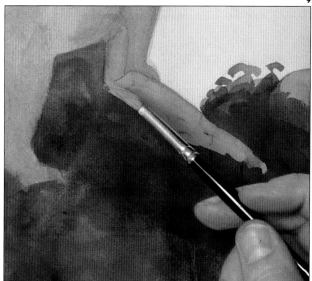

10

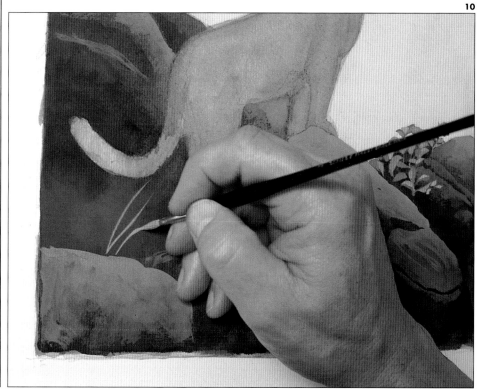

10 Next to receive attention are the areas of foliage. Mix together permanent green middle with brilliant yellow and a touch of white, and then use this to describe the leaves of the small plant on the right with a no. 3 sable brush. Start with a bias towards the permanent green middle, then paint further leaves with an equal mix of the three colours. This will give you two distinct shades of green that can then be blended and merged on the painting to create darker and lighter areas.

Reduce the amount of brilliant yellow in the mixture and then use this new shade to carefully paint the individual strands of grass over to the left. Lighten the mix slightly, and paint in some further strands and add the clump by the leopard's rear legs.

11 Mix a small amount of burnt umber with black, and continuing with your no. 2 sable brush, paint in the position of the spots on the leopard. Refer back to the reference as you go to make sure that these are as accurately placed as possible. This is only an early stage in the development of the leopard's coat. Later, you will cut in around these spots with a lighter colour, re-establishing their form in the finishing stages of the painting.

12 Add alizarin rose madder into your leopard spot mix and use it to build up the rocks. Keep your brush quite dry so that you are dragging the paint across the picture. By doing this the paint you put down will appear broken and scratchy which is perfect for depicting the rough surface texture of sun-baked rocks.

13   Now mix together your alizarin rose madder with some permanent white to create a pinky colour. Then, using a no. 6 sable brush, paint over the entire sky, cutting in, and so defining the outline, around the leopard as you go. You may find it easier to paint if you turn the painting sideways, as you can then run the brush down the skyline towards you. Alizarin has a bit of a reputation for creating uneven areas of flat colour, so you may have to give the sky a second coat once it has dried.

14   Return to your green mixture of permanent green middle, brilliant yellow and permanent white, but increase the amount of white to make it a lighter shade. Then use this to paint in some highlights on the plant to the right with your no. 3 brush. This completes the work to the background, and from now on you will concentrate on the leopard itself.

15   Switch back to your no. 2 sable brush for the remainder of this project. First, mix together a bit of permanent white, burnt umber and alizarin rose madder, and use this to cut in around the lower spots on the leopard. Then add yellow ochre into the mix for the more golden areas along the leopard's back. Adjust the mixture as you go and repaint

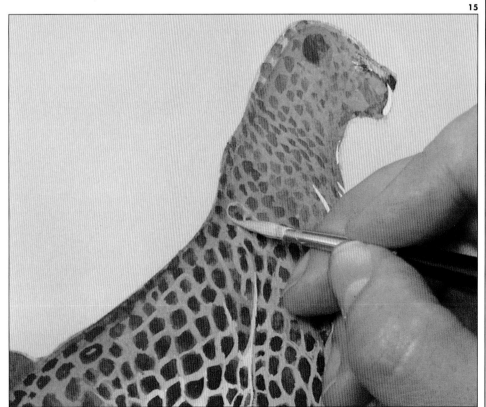

any areas that dry the wrong colour, constantly referring to the reference for guidance.

Whatever way your mix leans, remember to include a touch of alizarin rose madder to capture

the reflected light and retain the harmony of colours with the strong sunset sky.

16 Now add into the mix more permanent white and yellow ochre (the yellow ochre warms up the colour). This will make a much lighter and brighter gold colour that should be perfect for cutting in around the spots on the back of the leopard's neck and you can also use it to paint in the snout, ear and highlight on the cheek.

17 Blend a small amount of burnt umber into some black and use it to dot in the savage eyes and to repaint any of the spots which have become faded or spoilt due to you painting around them. Then use a very light mix of alizarin rose madder and permanent white to lighten up the tail and any other odd areas you feel may need it. Add yellow ochre into this mix to create a pale gold which you can use to paint the rest of the leopard's face, before finally switching to pure permanent white to paint in the whiskers.

18 To finish the painting, simply add a suggestion of green between the two front legs to separate them, use your lightest leopard tone to paint the feet, and then with a mixture of permanent white, alizarin rose madder, yellow ochre and a hint of burnt umber, paint in the middle splash of colour in the leopard's spots.

This type of project is a perfect example of the beauty of painting with gouache. Since it is a watercolour, the painting has traces of soft tone which are perfectly contrasted by the opaque colour painted over the top. The vibrancy of the colours lends itself to the subject matter, yet at the same time the paint is delicate enough to capture the smooth texture of the leopard's coat. In addition, this should have been a fairly simple project to follow. To have painted it with pure watercolour would have taken a good few hours of preparatory thought even to work out *how* to paint it, let alone to do the deed itself.

Falcons

ANIMALS

Often when people take up painting animals they assume that the easiest place to start is with their own pet. However, unless your pet happens to be a tortoise, it is unlikely that it will ever stay still long enough for you even to mix up your first colour. As illustrated in the previous project, photographic reference can be one solution, but here the artist found another. He went along to a natural history museum and found these wonderful stuffed falcons. As luck would have it, they were placed in a simple arrangement around a nest. Although the idea of stuffed animals may seem distasteful, it does allow you to study the subject at leisure and from any angle. With a photograph from a book you are limited to a single view.

Obviously, we are not suggesting that you always paint animals from photographs or museums, but they are a very good place to start since you can take your time without worrying whether the animal will move off. Once you are feeling a bit more confident, you could then try painting your own pet. After all, at some point, all artists will feel the urge to paint their loved one, be it cat, dog, hamster or canary (humans are covered in chapter 10).

The previous project introduced you to painting furry animals, so we will use these falcons to cover the feathery ones. People with slimy pets are evidently a bit strange and will not be pandered to in this book!

As we mentioned in the first paragraph, the museum had placed these birds in a simple arrangement. The triangle formed by the main branches and the top of the nest provides a linking element to the composition, taking the viewer's eye around the scene from one bird to the next. The background will be left blank to heighten the impact of the composition and to help the birds stand out. If you want to do a natural-looking painting of animals, it is important to place them in a relevant setting but, as shown here, this does not necessarily have to be very complicated.

In this painting, a more traditional approach associated with pure watercolour painting is used where the work is built up from light to dark, leaving the areas of white plumage and highlight as the white of the paper support. Only the final dramatic highlights are added in permanent white.

1   Stretch a sheet of heavy watercolour paper the day before you intend painting this project, and allow it to dry overnight. Since this is quite an intricate composition, mark out a detailed outline drawing with an HB pencil. Take your time, not only making sure that you capture the form of the birds correctly but also that of the myriad branches and twigs which make up their nest.

2   Start by laying thin washes of colour over the lightest areas. Use a no. 5 sable brush and a very watery mix of burnt sienna mixed with a little ivory black to block in the legs of the falcon on the left. Then add cobalt blue and a small amount of permanent white to turn the mixture into more of a blue/brown colour and, again with lots of water, lay a thin wash over the body of the nest, any twigs which stick out from it and the chick.

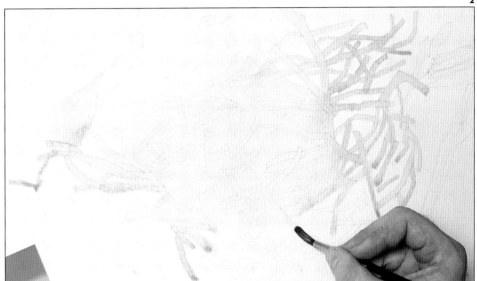

3   It is a good idea to pull the various elements in this picture together as soon as possible. This will then enable you to work on individual sections one at a time since you will not have blank expanses of paper upsetting the balance and putting you off. As the branches of the tree are this unifying element, they are your next area of attention.
  Mix burnt sienna, yellow ochre and a small amount of black to create dark brown. Then, still using quite a bit of water in your mix, paint in the form of the main branches. Do not worry if this runs into the other washes slightly as it will all add to the picture.

ANIMALS / FALCONS

4 Once you have painted the branches, allow your painting to dry so that you can attend to the falcon on the left without any worry of the paint merging. Create a very pale blue/grey tone by mixing together cobalt blue and ivory black with lots of water, and block in the shape of the bird. Its form will be built up later on by a process of overlaying washes (see page 49). However, make sure that you leave its breast and the front of its head unpainted since these contain areas of pure white.

5 Whilst the base colour of the falcon is drying you can do some further work to the nest. Recreate your branch mix of cobalt blue and ivory black, making it darker by decreasing the amount of water in the mix. Use this colour with a no. 2 sable brush to carefully paint

in the gaps between the various twigs which make up the nest. This technique of creating light areas by cutting in dark tones around them is very common in pure watercolour painting but works just as well with gouache. Because gouache can be painted opaque, the temptation is to lay a middle tone over the entire nest and then work the dark and light areas on top. However, this would mean painting quite extensive areas in opaque, and since opaque gouache is very chalky this could produce a hazy effect which would spoil the painting. In addition, the consistency of gouache is particularly suited for this cutting-in technique. Although the ability to paint with gouache in opaque is a bonus, it is easy to get into a routine and forget to be inventive.

6

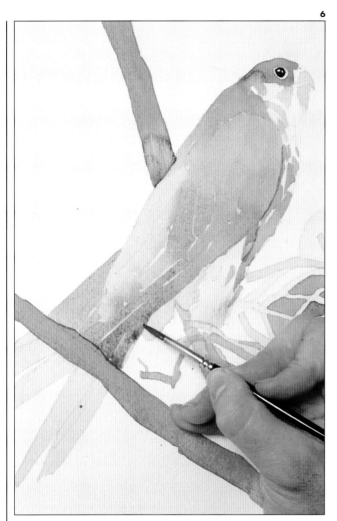

7

6 Returning to the falcon, paint in its eye with pure ivory black, and then add cobalt blue so that you return to the blue/grey mix you originally painted the bird with – but with a bias towards the blue. This time, do not add as much water so that the mix appears a bit darker. Use it to paint various areas on the bird so that you get distinctly different tones in its plumage. You can add further variety by including a little yellow ochre into your mix for small sections such as the tops of the wings.

7 Again, as the paint on the falcon dries, switch back to working on the nest and branches. You still want a dark brown colour, but this time use a mixture of ivory black with a small amount of yellow ochre added. By creating a slightly different dark-brown mix you will get colour and tonal variation in what would otherwise be rather 'flat' areas. Repaint various parts of the lower sections of the branches and the nest. This will help suggest the areas in partial shadow towards the bottom of the picture and create a range of texture in the wood.

8 It is now a good idea to do some work on the falcon to the right before it gets left too far behind. As with the first falcon, it is built up by overlaying washes of your blue/grey mixture. But, since its white, speckled breast is towards the viewer, there is no initial stage of blocking in its whole form. In fact its plumage is suggested more by dashes of colour, with the only really dark patches on its head and down its wings. Do not forget to dot in its eye with some pure ivory black.

8

9

10

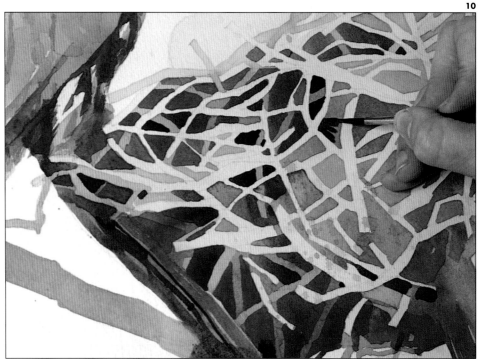

9 Switch to a no. 1 sable brush for the final areas of blue/grey colour to the falcons. Paint little dabs of this colour over the darkest areas of the birds' plumage to suggest the slightly uneven texture of fine feathers and down the tail feathers where the fine veins can be seen.

11

12

10 Continuing with your no. 1 sable brush, create a watery mix of ivory black and indicate the texture of the bark on the branches by painting thin, delicate lines running along them. Luckily ivory black is quite a brown-black so it is perfect for this painting. Next, mix some burnt sienna into your black to create a dark brown and use this tone to darken down most, but not all, of the gaps between the twigs of the nest.

11 Now use a watery mix of golden yellow to paint in the eyes of all the birds, the feet of the falcon on the right, and the details around the beaks of the other falcon and the chick. Then switch to ivory black with only a small amount of water added to finish the modelling on the two adult birds' heads. Paint with small dashes to capture the effect of very fine plumage. Once you are happy that you have added enough detail, stop and allow the painting to dry thoroughly.

12 When you are sure that the painting has dried, use your HB pencil to draw fine lines on both the adult birds to give the impression of the downy feathers on their breasts and the veins in their tail feathers and along the large feathers on the back of the falcon to the left.

13 If you had done this painting in pure watercolour the previous step would have concluded the work to the adult falcons.

However, as you should know by now, gouache can be painted opaque. This means that you can now go back and paint some highlights in the birds' plumage.

Use your no. 1 sable brush and a fairly thick mix of permanent white to add small dashes of highlight between some of the pencil marks you made in the last step. Pay particular attention

13

to the form of the birds, only adding these highlights where they would be present – such as at the top of the wing of the left-hand falcon.

14 To finish the painting, simply mix yellow ochre and cobalt blue with a lot of water, and use a no. 5 sable brush to add a wash over the body of the little chick. Then at last you can step back and appraise your work. Although you did in fact use some opaque gouache, since it was kept to a minimum and only introduced in the finishing stages, the painting has all the delicate translucency of one rendered in pure watercolour.

Hopefully this project will have given you an insight into painting not just falcons, but

all our feathered friends. Since most birds have plumage consisting of one predominant colour, the process of building up tone by overlaying washes is especially useful. In addition, you should not be afraid to switch to a graphite pencil to add the fine veins present on larger feathers. Not only does pencil complement gouache quite nicely but, as shown in this project, it can also provide a guide for adding fine opaque highlights over the top. You must remember that there is really no such thing as cheating in art. If something works for you – be it mixing your media, tracing your reference or whatever – then it is permissible. Remember, you are supposed to be enjoying yourself!

14

Chapter 9
Still Life

Still life has always been a popular subject in Western Art. Examples have even been found in the ruins of Pompeii. However, due to the power of the Christian Church, when still life reappeared in the Renaissance, it played only a minor part in the iconography of religious paintings – various objects were used to complement and explain a religious or mythological theme. With the rise of the middle classes and the division of the Church in the 17th century, still life became an extremely popular subject in its own right.

Today, still lifes are seen as decorative, uncontroversial paintings, which are fun to paint because of the control you have over your subject matter. A still life provides the perfect model – motionless with a never-ending range of shapes, form, textures and colour. In addition, you can change the arrangement as you wish, really taking your time over it. You can set it up, work on it for as long as you like, leave it and then come back to it over and over again. You, the artist, are in complete control.

In this chapter we break you in gently with a very simple arrangement of tulips lying on a sheet of paper. The whole painting is created by the use of overlaying washes in only a few basic mixes. The second project also makes use of a limited palette, but it is a much more ambitious affair. So pick up your brushes and start painting straightaway.

Tulips

STILL LIFE

For this still-life project, we originally decided to depict the classic subject of a vase of flowers. However, when the artist returned from the florist and started to open the paper, the telephone rang and he rushed to answer it. On his return, he loved the way the tulips had fallen, so instead of putting them in water he photographed them there and then. Apart from making an unusual change, the overall composition had a much more natural feel.

You may be wondering why they had to be photographed and could not be painted from life. The incident with the telephone happened in the evening, and the photographer for this book, as well as ourselves, had gone home. The artist realized that the likelihood of such a perfect arrangement recurring was remote. Even so, the tulips proved to be a bit of a problem to photograph because they sprawled over quite a large area and the artist needed a fairly close-up shot to work from so he would not lose any of the details. To overcome this – as you can see below – he took two shots, one of each side, and taped them together.

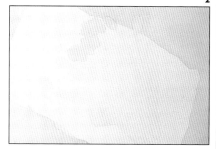

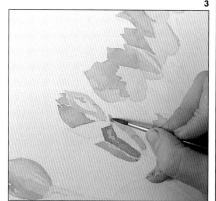

1 Using an HB pencil lay down your initial sketch. This must be as light as possible – to avoid it showing through in the finished painting – so do not be tempted to press too hard on the paper. Once you are happy with your sketch, mix some lemon yellow and permanent green light with lots of water to create a pale wash. Using a no. 2 sable brush paint this mix over the leaves and stems of the tulips.

2 You are now going to move on to the flower heads. Mix together some rose carthame with a touch of lemon yellow and, once again, lots of water. The addition of lemon yellow may sound a little strange, but it is used to create a slightly more orange tone, which is needed for the flowers. Rinse the no. 2 brush, and use it to lay this first wash over the heads of the flowers. Switching to a no. 8 brush and a fresh, watery mix of cool grey no. 3 and indigo, lay down the background wash.

3 This painting is built up in layers, by overpainting each element with a darker mix than the previous one. This is mainly achieved by using the same colours, but with a higher ratio of pigment to water. Switching back to the no. 2 sable brush and with your original mix of rose carthame and a little lemon yellow, but much less water, start to paint in the darker shades of the petals to add more shape and definition to the heads of the flowers.

4 Although you have already started to overpaint the flower heads, the stems and leaves still need to be worked on with another watery mix. This is because they contain a wider variety of tones than the flowers. Mix some sap green and primary blue with lots of water and start to define the shapes of the leaves and their mid-tone shadows, constantly referring back to the original reference photographs.

5 Back to the flowers, and with the same mix of rose carthame, lemon yellow and hardly any water at all, overpaint the darker shades of the flower heads once again. To increase their three-dimensionality, mix a little cobalt blue with some geranium and very little water, to create a purple shade. With a well-loaded brush, drip this into the wet paint so that it spreads out over the surface to add slightly more texture and a softer effect.

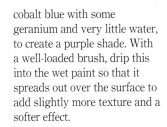

6 Now, back once again to the stems and leaves. With the mix of sap green, primary blue and very little water, paint in the darker shadows on the leaves. Add some raw umber to the mix – to make it even darker – and locate the small areas of darkest shadow and carefully paint them in. All this overpainting may seem a touch unnecessary, but as you can see the tulips are by now looking really lifelike.

7 This should really be your final stage of work to the tulips, as all that remains are the fine details on the petals. Switching to a no. 1 sable brush and with your usual mix of rose carthame, lemon yellow and practically no water, start to paint in – very carefully – fine lines along and across the flower petals to give them more form.

8 The leaves are still in need of a little more definition, but you can change back to your no. 3 sable brush, as this task does not involve such fine details. Re-create your usual green mix, but this time make the ratio of primary blue higher than the sap green, and add in a little alizarin crimson which will darken the colour. Paint this over the darkest shadows to bring them forward. Switching to a no. 8 sable brush, mix some ivory black, cobalt blue and lots of water, and loosely block in the background so that the white of the paper really stands out.

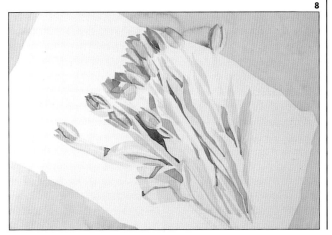

9 At this stage it is a good idea to stand back and take an overall look at your painting. Although it looks almost finished, when gouache colour dries on the paper it has a tendency to look much flatter and lighter than when it is wet, which has happened here. Therefore you will need to go over the tulips once more. This time do not add any water to the rose carthame and lemon yellow mixture and just pick out the darkest areas only. Repeat this on the leaves, again with no water added to the green leaf mix from step 8.

10 The tulips should by now look perfect, so this really is the final stage. With the same mix that you used for the background – but with a higher ratio of indigo than ivory black, and lots of water added – you can now tackle the shadows on the crinkly paper. Paint all the light shadows first, then add some geranium into the mix for the darker ones behind the flower heads. You may think this addition of colour is rather strange, but because the paper is so white the shadows also reflect the colour of the flowers.

11 At last you can stand back and admire your work. Never be put off if your painting does not look exactly the same as the one in our picture as these step-by-steps are merely a guide to help you to familiarize yourself with the medium. However, even though overpainting the same areas again and again might have felt repetitive, you cannot deny that the end result made it all worth while. With every fresh layer of paint, the tulips took on a more three-dimensional form, and as an end result they really come out of the picture, making you feel that you could almost pick them up.

9

10

11

117

CDs

STILL LIFE

Here you have an interesting project – a very modern subject painted in a rather traditional style. The fact that it works so well shows that you really can include anything in a still-life composition. So often people think of still lifes as just involving potted plants, cut flowers and bowls of fruit, but in truth anything will do. Sometimes it is best to wander around your house until an object or a group of objects catches your eye, and then just sit down and paint it as it stands – this is called a 'found' still life. However, this project is an example of an 'artificial' still life. This is where you collect your objects together and arrange them in a group, also arranging the background, lighting, viewpoint, etc. In short, you totally create a setting which you will then paint.

In this case the objects were selected to provide you with some interesting textures to paint – the matt finish of the CD player, the plastic cases and the eerie metallic sheen of the CDs themselves. In addition, it is logical for the items to be together so this gives the scene a natural sense of harmony.

Since the objects are so obviously man-made and modern, the artist decided to use a slow and considered approach so that their form could be captured accurately. A loose base of washes is created first which is then used as a guide for carefully applying the opaque paint on top. This is the traditional way of working in gouache, and in many respects is one of the most satisfactory since you get quite a solid feel, yet at the same time retain some of the delicacy of pure watercolour.

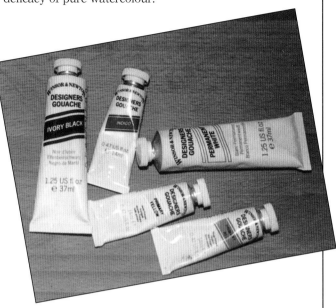

1 Having stretched a sheet of watercolour paper the day before (see page 42 for full instructions on how to do this), start by roughing out your initial outline sketch with a 2B pencil. Take your time, paying particular attention to the way that the CDs are distorted into ellipses from this viewpoint.

2 Use a large wash brush to lay some water over the paper. This will hopefully create some interesting effects when the paint is applied. With a no. 6 Series 7 sable brush lay in the dark background tone of ivory black mixed with primary red and indigo blue. Switch to a no. 3 brush for the more fiddly

areas and to suggest the form of the singer on the front of the CD case.

3 Whilst this first wash dries, mix together indigo blue, primary red and primary yellow and water to create a pale wash for the open CD case. Turn this into a more

orange hue by increasing the amount of primary red, and then paint in the shape of the guitar held by the singer. You can then paint the dark surround on the interior of the open CD case by adding ivory black into your mix so that it appears similar to the background tone.

4   What you are doing in these initial stages is to block in with dilute colour before you start to work in opaque. This not only gives you a basic mid-tone to work from, but also allows you to cover the whole picture at a very early stage – so establishing the 'mood'.

All these base tones are created from the same three colours – blue, red and yellow sometimes with the addition of ivory black – you simply adjust the mix to suit the object. Now add a suggestion of the forms on the CD covers, increasing the amount of primary red for the orange areas, and reducing the yellow for the pale purple tones. You can also use this pale purple tone to paint in the remaining sections of the CD cases.

5   For the CDs themselves, virtually remove all trace of indigo blue from the basic mix, and reduce the amount of primary red so that you arrive at a very pale orange. Use this, with a lot of water, to block in the CD at the front. Slightly increase the amount of primary red and indigo blue so that the colour 'muddies' and darkens a bit, and then paint in the other CD. You can also use this hue to establish the small area of light floor visible on the right.

6   The CD player can now be blocked in. Return to an equal mix of all three colours and add in a small amount of ivory black to create a mid-grey tone. Increase or decrease the amount of water in the mix as you paint the CD player so that you get an area of uneven tone. For the LED panel, add in lots more indigo blue and a bit more primary red so that the mix turns into a deep purple.

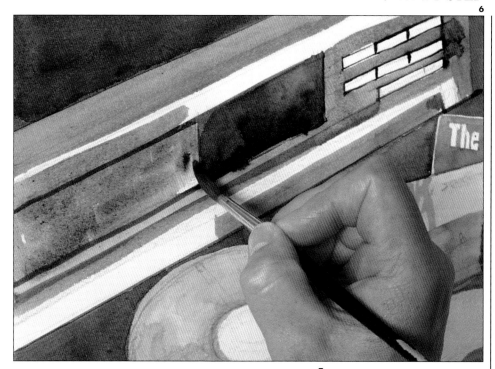

7   Finally, re-create the initial mix and use it to further darken the background down and to add the dark holes in the centres of the CDs. All the base tones have now been established so take a break whilst the painting dries.

   Before you start over-painting with opaque colour, clean your palette for a fresh start. Mix together some primary red, primary yellow and permanent white (to make the mix more opaque) and paint the inside lid of the open CD case. Start at the top and as you work down towards the bottom add a small amount of indigo blue into the mix. This maintains the basic colour, but makes it appear as if light is falling across the area.

8

9

10

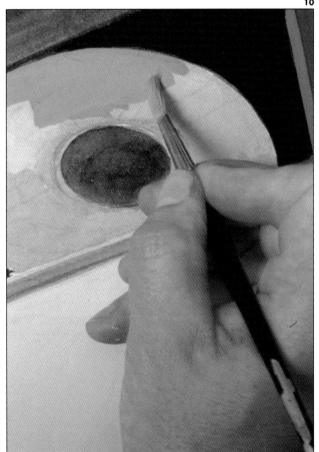

8   Next to be worked up is the dark plastic visible on the open CD case. Since you are using the three primary colours, when you mix them together in equal amounts they form black. So, by adding a small amount of permanent white, it is easy to arrive at a good dark grey tone which is perfect for the plastic.

9   Continue by marking out the detail on the two CD covers. Here especially your underpainting will prove to be worth its weight in gold. Simply recreate the tones you originally painted, but this time in opaque. You can obviously check the reference photograph for further inspiration, but try not to get too carried away in adding fine details. A general suggestion of form is amply sufficient.

Once you have finished the covers, return to the dark grey mix for the plastic strip down the spine of the John Lee Hooker CD.

10   For the CDs themselves, use primary red, primary yellow and permanent white with only a small amount of indigo blue added to arrive at a neutral colour with a slight tinge of violet. Adjust the mix as you go to create variations in tone, especially on the CD at the back where a dark band can be added to suggest the shadows falling on it.

11 Now you can concentrate on the CD player. Start by using the CD mix from the previous step to paint the very lightest tones present. Since this is such an angular object with harsh edges and sharp corners, it is a good idea to use a ruler so that you get crisp lines. This is an easy technique to master (see page 55 for detailed instructions), as you simply run the metal ferrel of your brush along the upturned edge of the ruler and you have a perfect straight line. The remainder of the CD player is made up of dark grey tones, so mix equal amounts of your three colours to create a black and then add in a small amount of permanent white. Paint in all the darkest areas first and then lighten your mixture by adding in some more white. Repeat this process until you have painted the entire CD player.

11

12

12 To finish the work to the CD player, now turn to the LEDs. Although this includes some fiddly detail, it is important that you do not paint the numbers too big (as you would not be able to fit them all in), so it is wise to plot their position carefully in pencil first. The panel is very dark so these pencil marks will be unlikely to show through in the finished painting. Mix together primary red, primary yellow and permanent white to create a pale orange tone, and carefully mark in the LEDs with a no. 3 sable brush.

13 As you can see from the reference photograph, when light falls on a CD it creates weird rays of colour across its surface – a similar effect to a rainbow. You can accentuate these in the painting to heighten the impact of the CDs. Create a pale blue by mixing a tiny dot of indigo blue with a lot of permanent white, and paint some rays with the aid of a ruler. Next include some pale green rays by adding a small amount of primary yellow into your pale blue mix. Finally add in pale pink rays by mixing a speck of primary red with a lot of white. You can then paint the rays on the other CD by adding a small amount of primary yellow into your pink mixture so that it turns into a pale orange.

14

14 Before you wipe the pale orange tone from your palette, use it to speck in the detailing on the middle of both the exposed CDs with a no. 3 Series 7 sable brush. The Series 7 is so named because Queen Victoria was a keen watercolour artist and her favourite brush was a no. 7 from Winsor and Newton. Consequently they named a whole range of brushes the Series 7 to honour this fact.

15 All that is needed now to finish the painting is the lettering on the exposed CD at the front. As with the LEDs which you painted earlier, it is definitely a good idea to plot these letters out in pencil before you start with the paint. Mix together indigo blue, primary yellow and only a touch of primary red so that you get a rather dirty green hue, and then again using the no. 3 brush, block in the lettering.

16 You have now completed the painting so you can step back and allow it to dry. Notice how, although the painting looks fairly detailed, any intricate areas such as the writing on the open CD case have been ignored. It is important you realize that unless you want to create photo-realistic paintings, then a certain amount of detail will always have to be dropped. By taking your time on the LEDs and the large writing on the CD, you create the impression of a highly worked painting without actually doing very much.

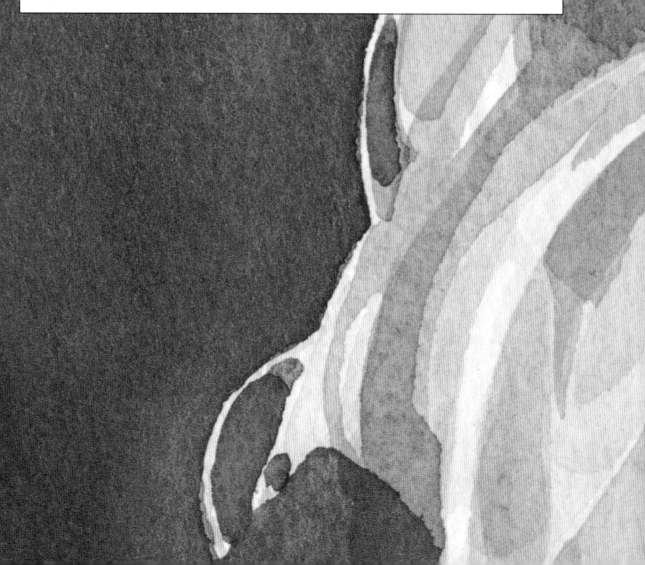

Chapter 10
The Human Figure

Perhaps the most challenging subject of all is the human figure – be it full figure or portrait. Painting the human figure is an age-old, traditional theme for the artist, and so there is an abundance of examples to give you inspiration, dating right back to the cave paintings of prehistoric man. The fact that painting the human figure has never gone out of fashion implies that there is an instinctive desire in humans to want to depict themselves.

Although we may all appear to be similar, everyone is in truth unique. Anatomists talk of the 'normal' proportions of the body, but most people differ from this at least in one respect. In addition our varying bone structure and musculature make us yet more individual, and when it comes to facial features... well, unless you have an identical twin, you are definitely unique in this respect. Therefore, due to this huge variety in subject matter, painting the human figure can be a lifetime's enjoyment in itself.

We start with a portrait of a young girl and explore the process of building up skin tones through subtle layers of paint. The second project is of a group of figures in varying poses and is an exercise in exploring the opacity of gouache for flesh tones and the surrounding scenery. If you follow both projects carefully you will be well on the way to understanding how to paint the human figure.

Alice

THE HUMAN FIGURE

Although this little girl looks like she belongs in a 'Saint Trinians' film, she is in fact the artist's daughter. By plying her with promises of sweets, he managed to make her stay still long enough to take a photograph – ten seconds in one place seems to be about her maximum, so all our thanks go out to the inventor of the camera.

A great deal of emphasis is placed on the fact that, since gouache can be painted opaque, you can work from dark to light, but with a portrait such rigid conventions do not really apply. Instead a more sensible approach is to start in the centre and let the painting grow out from there. This allows you to build the portrait up slowly, which in turn enables you to concentrate on capturing the likeness.

Skin tones are one of the hardest things to master in any medium, and using gouache is no exception. However, you do have the advantage of being able to use very pale washes, wet-in-wet, wet-on-dry and pure opaque paint – a combination which gives you excellent control over your painting. The trick with skin tones is to build them up gradually, stopping the moment they are right, as, if they are overworked, they can look dull and dead – only really suitable if you fancy painting ghosts!

In this project the artist starts by laying an overall base tone, then builds up slowly with mixes containing very little water painted on already dry paint. This gives a wonderfully graphic interpretation which is easy to follow – the perfect introduction to the genre of portraiture.

1   As with most of the projects in this book, start by making a light pencil outline on some stretched paper. These must be kept very light so as not to show through the finished painting. As mentioned in the introduction

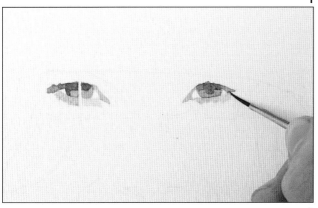

to this project you are going to work from the centre out, so concentrate on the eyes first. With this appealing subject, her eyes are going to be the focus of attention so it is important that they are perfect. Using a no. 1 sable brush and a very watery mix of Prussian blue and black, paint in the pupils. Then with cadmium red mixed with black, paint in the underside of the upper eye lids and then the lower lids, finally darkening the mix with more black for the shadow areas on the top lids and pupils.

2   Next, mix together cadmium red with yellow ochre and a little bit of black with quite a lot of water to create a light skin tone, and with a no. 2 sable brush wash thinly over the rest of the face. Change the mix slightly as you go to create variations in this basic tone. This establishes an all-over light skin tone which will be worked up later on.

3   Continuing with slight variations of the same basic mixture, but switching to a no. 8 sable brush, block in the

rest of the skin tone for the body and then allow it to dry. Now paint a very dark flesh tone – a mix of cadmium red, yellow ochre and small amounts of black and Prussian blue (the blue is used to darken it) – over the face, just leaving the highlight areas on the chin, lips and nose unpainted. You need to also paint the shadow area on the body with this tone. As you do this, tilt the painting slightly towards you so that the paint collects towards the bottom of the painted areas. This is perfect for these shadows since it emphasizes the harsh contrast at their edge.

4   Add golden yellow and permanent white to your dark skin tone and use it to define the contours of the face, switching back to your no. 2 sable brush so that you will have more control over the paint. Alter the mix as you go to create areas of light and dark tone until you arrive at the desired result. Then darken your mix right down with still more black and Prussian blue so that you can paint in the nostrils with a fairly dry brush.

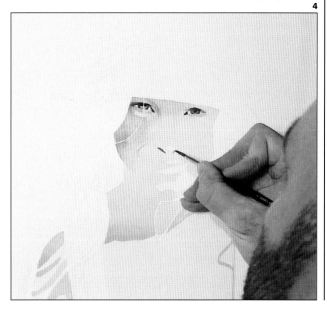

5

5   Now you will need a base colour for the hair. You paint this with yellow ochre mixed with a little bit of natural umber, using a no. 5 sable brush, and adding a bit of cadmium red to create the darker tones. Allow the paint to run down the tilted board to create quite a loose effect. If any drops of paint run too far down the painting, simply pick them off with a piece of tissue. Once all the hair has received its base coat leave the painting to dry.

6   Mix ivory black, burnt sienna and a little Prussian blue with lots of water and use this to paint the shadows in the texture of the hat using a no. 5 sable brush. Then add a bit of yellow ochre and paint the strip along the bottom lip of the hat. This is because the neutral coloured hat reflects local colours which is especially obvious on its bottom edge and the underside where it picks up the colour of the hair. Once the hat has completely dried you can then repaint the darker areas of the hair with a deeper mix of your original hair colour.

7   Continuing with your no. 5 sable brush, darken down your hair mixture even further by adding some black into the mixture, and pick out the darker tones in the hair. The building up of the hair is a gradual process which should not be rushed. At each stage darken the mix a little further, and decrease the area you are painting. Eventually you will end up with a very dark tone which you will paint in only one or two isolated areas to represent the very darkest shadows – notably under the hat and around the face.

6

7

8 To break the routine a bit, you can now turn to the dungarees. To start with, you will find it easier if you lay a flat wash of heavily diluted cobalt blue over both the braces and the top of the bib with a no. 8 sable brush. Once this has dried (and this is the perfect time to make use of a hairdryer), use a much neater mix of your cobalt blue to add the detailing down the braces and the shadows around the fastenings.

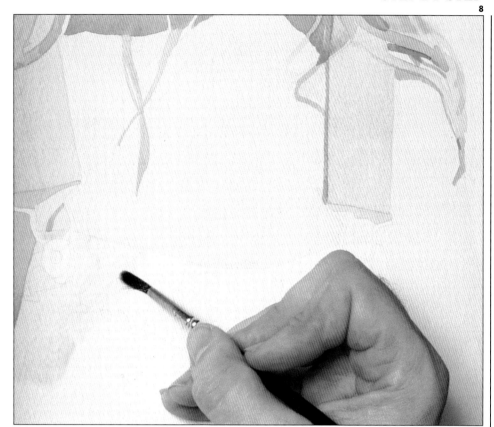

9 Returning to the face, recreate your dark skin tone mix of cadmium red, yellow ochre, golden yellow, permanent white, black and Prussian blue and continue with the modelling, paying particular attention to the form of the nose. Now add the details – the lips need a layer of very watered-down cadmium red. To pick out the eyelashes, use your very darkest skin tone mix and a no. 1 sable brush for maximum control. You will find that you need to keep reworking the face because gouache dries so much lighter than it appears when wet. It is therefore hard to judge the dry colour and so it is a good idea to work up the areas of skin tone slowly, building it up through multiple layers until you get the result you want.

10

11

10 Increase the amount of cadmium red in your dark skin tone and then repaint the neck and the face, taking care to isolate and leave unpainted the highlights on the nose, the top lip, under the eyes and on the chin. This will give the skin a more healthy glow and increase the contrast between the dark and light areas. Then add a small dab of watery cadmium red to the nose and the lips – again to liven up the colours a bit. Whilst this dries you can concentrate on the underside of the hat. Paint this with a dark blue mix created from black and cobalt blue with a no. 5 sable brush, not forgetting the thin strips of colour showing through between the strands of hair.

Hopefully by now the face will have dried, so you can return to it to add the freckles. These were not actually present on the model, but such artistic licence will improve the painting, adding interest around the nose area. They are very easy to include – simply add more yellow ochre into your dark skin tone and dot them in using the point of a no. 5 sable brush.

11 The painting is now virtually finished, so a background tone can be added to set the portrait off. In this case a dark, nondescript colour was selected so as to not detract from the little girl's face. Mix olive green with black and roughly paint in around the hat and the hair with a large soft brush, such as a no. 12, but switch to a finer brush (your no. 5 will be ideal) for the fiddly bits where the background tone abuts the figure.

12 The background tone should be re-painted a couple of times to give the colour depth and to ensure that, when dry, it is sufficiently dark, yet does not sit as a flat block of solid tone. As a final touch, paint the dark line between the lips with your no. 1 sable brush and a fairly dry mix of black and cadmium red.

13 Once your painting has fully dried you will be able to inspect it and see if any areas need touching up or if any colours have dried too light. These can then be quickly attended to.

As you can see, as predicted the eyes are certainly the focus of attention and so it was wise to start with them. You will notice that, moving out from the eyes, less and less detail has been included, until you reach the amorphous background tone and the fading out of the subject at the bottom. This intentional lack of interest at the edges of the painting ensures that the viewer's attention is always drawn back to the face and so, in turn, the eyes. It is wise to pay attention to the eyes in any portrait you paint as they invariably do most to reveal the subject's character and so will always attract maximum criticism. In fact, if you get the eyes right, people are far less likely to notice any other faults the painting may have.

12

The Bathers

THE HUMAN FIGURE

For this figure study we decided on a complete contrast to the previous project of a true-to-life portrait. Here we not only depict a group of figures, but also illustrate how you can create the human form successfully without paying attention to facial details. This painting also shows how to exploit the opaque property of the medium, which is the very nature of gouache. Although this is primarily an exercise in creating flesh tones, it shows us how, by dry brushing light over dark, the most wonderful textures can be achieved, such as in the rocks and the sea.

As we have already mentioned, an artist will very rarely venture out on a trip without his or her sketch book, or, for ease and convenience, a camera. This particular day was no exception for our artist, who was on holiday in Italy and visiting the seaside town of Positano. As he strolled around the coast, he came upon this charming scene of some young girls bathing from the rocks. He felt that it summed up the lazy, relaxing atmosphere of his Mediterranean holiday and if he made a painting of it on his return, it would bring back happy memories. At least this is his story, but his wife maintains that it was just an excuse to take a lot of pictures of pretty young girls! Whatever the reason, his judgement was correct in that it does work beautifully as a painting.

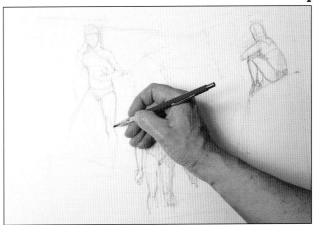

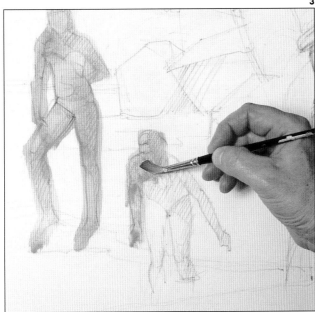

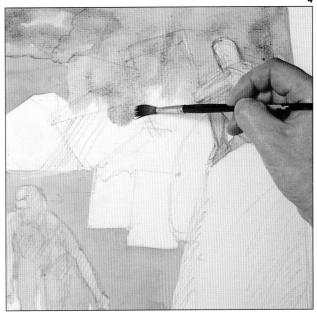

1 Due to the fact that the painting for this project is composed from three different photographs, it is important to make a thumbnail sketch first to plot out the scene exactly. If you do not do this and try to work directly from all three photographs, you may find the scene does not come together and ends up looking confused. With a 2B graphite pencil map out where the figures will be and in which poses and outline the shape and form of the rocks. When you are happy with the scene, you might decide to crop the picture for added drama.

2 Using the same soft pencil, transfer your chosen scene onto some stretched paper. Do not be tempted to save time and go straight to this stage. The thumbnail sketch can be altered or drawn several times until you are satisfied that it is right, whereas once you start to mark the support any changes that are made or rubbed out will break the surface of the paper. This could leave you with a bit of a mess which, in turn, could ruin an expensive piece of paper. Make your initial pencil drawing fairly detailed, roughly shading in the

shadows in the background and the darker tones of the flesh on the three figures.

3 Once you are happy with the pencil sketch, you can start blocking in with paint. For this first step mix some yellow ochre, cadmium red pale and lots of water to create a light wash for the flesh tones. With a no. 6 Series 7 sable brush lay this base colour over all three figures, including their swimming costumes and hair. Even though these parts are obviously not flesh-coloured it does not matter as superimposed layers of

gouache will cover the areas completely.

4 The next mix of paint is for the sea, and is made up from Prussian blue, permanent green middle and again lots of water. Lay this wash over the area of sea, darkening it slightly with a little extra Prussian blue where the sea deepens. Moving over to the rocks, mix some Prussian blue, cadmium red pale and yellow ochre with plenty of water and roughly wash it over the rocks, varying the mix as you go by pulling in more of one or other of the colours.

THE HUMAN FIGURE / THE BATHERS

5 When you are happy with the rocks, wash the same mix evenly over the whole area of the sea, including the rock that the two figures are bathing from. This will darken the sea and, although it is not as dark in the original photographs, we decided to use a bit of 'poetic licence' to add more drama to the finished painting. To this wash add a little more of each of the three colours, but no more water, and paint over the darker areas of the rocks in the background and the dark shadows. To paint the large rock in the foreground loosely mix some yellow ochre, Prussian blue and burnt umber with less water than you have been using previously. Keep this mix fairly loose and scumble the colours together on the support rather than on the palette so that you get quite a broken tone.

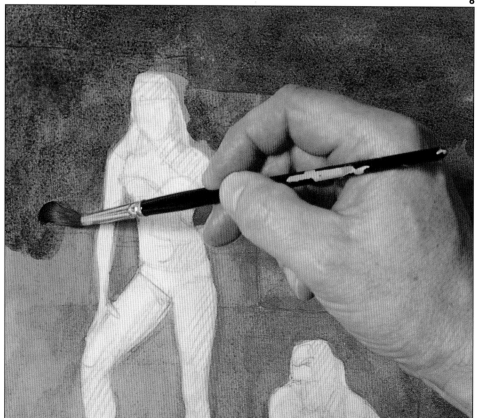

6 You are now going to work on the sea, but before you do this add some more water to the rock mix and wash this over the whole of the sea area again. This is not only to darken the sea, it is also because the rocks run under the sea and therefore create shadows in the water. The next mix is for the sea and consists of Prussian blue and permanent green middle with some water. Lay this wash over the whole of the sea and then wash it over the rocks. This may sound strange, but by covering these two areas – the rocks and the sea – in the same wash you will create a sense of harmony in the picture.

7

7   At this stage, having laid all the foundation washes of colour, you can step back and get a good overall feel for your painting before working up specific areas. The sea should not need any further work but the rocks are far from complete. Mix together some yellow ochre, burnt umber, Prussian blue and permanent white, and do not add any water. First, test that the rock area is quite dry, then dry-brush your mix over the rocks to create texture, adding a little more yellow ochre for extra warmth to those areas which reflect the sunlight.

8   Now you can concentrate on the figures. With a mix of cadmium red pale, yellow ochre, burnt umber, Prussian blue and water, carefully paint in the dark shadows, modelling the flesh of the two figures on the right. Darken this mix by adding more Prussian blue to paint in the bikini and the swimming costume. Now paint in the hair using the same mix. Note how a small area has been left unpainted on the head of the central figure, allowing the white paper to show through and thus creating the highlight where the sun is reflected in the hair.

9   This stage is really a repeat of the previous step, as it involves working on the standing figure on the left. Start with a mix of cadmium red pale, yellow ochre, burnt umber, Prussian blue and water to add the dark shadows on the flesh. Darken this mix with Prussian blue and paint in the hair, once again leaving a small area for the highlight.

8

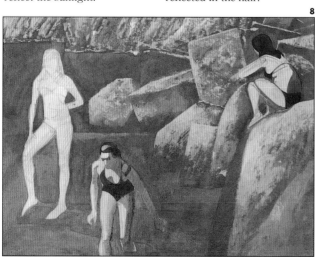

9

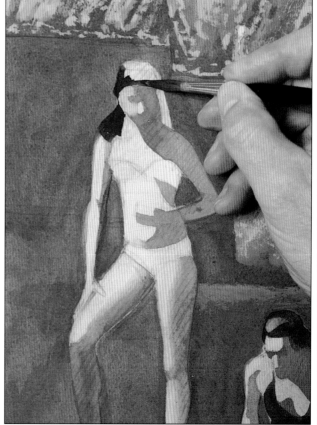

THE HUMAN FIGURE / THE BATHERS

10 The figures are really starting to come alive, but their flesh does not look tanned enough. To darken the skin, mix a dilute wash of yellow ochre and cadmium red pale and lay it over all three figures. Unfortunately, in this case, it made them look a little too tanned, so a small amount of burnt umber and Prussian blue was added to re-create the original flesh tone and the figures were painted again.

11 Mix all the colours on your palette together, with no extra water, and darken the rock from which the two bathers are swimming. Now mix burnt umber, Prussian blue, permanent green middle and plenty of water to wash into the sea in the foreground. Vary the mix as you go to show that the rock continues beneath the surface of the water. With a fresh mix of permanent white, a little Prussian blue, permanent green middle and hardly any water, start to add the foam.

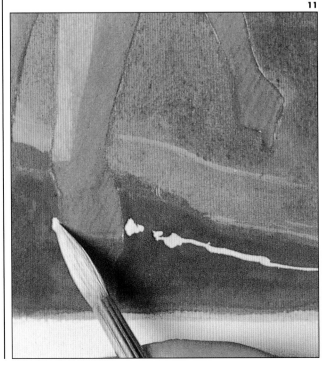

12 Continue to add the foam, varying the mix slightly with the addition of a little extra colour. Then move back to the figure on the left as she still has no bikini. Mix a tiny amount of cobalt blue and white to paint in the background tone and then mix the same amount of cadmium red pale with white to add the floral pattern.

138

13   All the painting needs now is some finishing touches on the figures. This is simply a matter of adding some highlights to the flesh to really bring the girls alive. With a mix of cadmium red pale, yellow ochre, permanent white and hardly any water, start to paint in the light tones along the front of the legs for the central figure, the sides of the legs for the crouching figure and on the legs and arms of the figure on the left, as well as around her hand to give more definition.

14   As you stand back and admire your work you will be able to see what a difference these last highlights make to the figures. It is also worth noting that none of the facial features were painted in any detail, but merely suggested with the use of shadows and highlights. As you can see, this has worked perfectly and is almost a trick played by the artist on the viewer. This is because we know in our minds that they have eyes, noses, etc, and therefore we see them. This painting again shows how versatile a medium gouache is. Because it is a form of watercolour it can be diluted with lots of water to create subtle washes, and yet neat – as in the foam on the sea and highlights on the flesh – you can see how successfully you can paint light over dark yet still achieve a subtle end result.

Index

A

Abstract, dictionary definition 84
Abstract expressionism 84
Abstracting a real scene 86
Acrylic paint 62, 63
Action painting 84
Advertisements as inspiration 20
Airbrushing 16
Albani, Francesco 13
Alice 128-33
Architecture 76
'Artificial' still life 118

B

Balla, Giacomo 16
Barraband, Jacques 13
Bathers 134-9
Bauhaus 14
Blanc fixe 32
Blending 48, 50, 77, 100
Blon, Le 26
Boccioni, Umberto 16
Botticelli, Sandro 14
Braque, Georges 15, 16
Brickwork 90
Bristle brushes 36, 55
Brush ruling 55, 83, 95, 123
Brushes 36-7
 bristles 36, 55
 camel hair 36
 Chinese hog hair 36
 cleaning 36-7
 control 60, 64, 74
 natural hair 36
 rolling 65
 sable 36
 squirrel
Building up tone 49, 52
Burne-Jones, Sir Edward 14

C

Camel hair brushes 36
Cameras 20, 58, 128
Cardboard 34
CDs 118-25
Centre of vision 24, 25
Ceramic palettes 39
Cézanne, Paul 15, 27
Chinese hog hair brushes 36

Choosing your subject 20
Cleaning brushes 36-7
Cold Colours 28
Cold Pressed paper 34
Color-field 16
Colour 26-9
 blending 48
 fading 32
 halo 51
 harmony 26, 58, 61, 100
 intensity 70
Coloured papers 34
Coloured pencils 93
Complementary Colours 26-8
Composition 22, 106
Cotman brushes 37
Cox, David 14, 15
Creating texture 54
Cubism 15, 16
Cutting-in 64, 66, 103, 104, 108

D

Dabbing with tissue 77
De Stijl 14
Degas, Edgar 13
Design 22-4
Diluting paint 44-5
Distorting viewpoint 119
Doesburg, Theo Van 14, 15
Drawing boards 39, 42-3
Dropping wet-in-wet 51
Dry brushing 55, 60, 61, 102, 137
Drying 73
Dürer, Albrecht 13
Dyck, Sir Anthony Van 13

E

Easels 39
Egyptian papyrus 35
Egyptian Village 86-91
Ellsworth, Roy 23, 25
Erotic painting 12, 13
Eye-level viewpoint 24

F

Fading colours 32
Falcons 106-11
Fixative 77
Flat wash 46

Flint, Sir William Russell 14, 15
'Found' still life 118
French Fishing Boats 70-5
French Impressionists 14

G

Geometric design 22-4
Golden section 22-4
Goupy, Joseph 12
Gradation of tone 47, 51
Graded wash 47
Grandison, William 16, 17
Graphite pencils 39, 75
Guazzo 12
Gum arabic 32
Gum tragacanth 32
Gummed paper 42-3

H

Hardboard 34
Hepworth, Barbara 16
Highlights 52, 53, 55, 81, 82, 103, 111, 139
Hilliard, Nicholas 12, 13
Horizon line 24, 25
Hot Pressed paper 34
Human Figure, full figure 134-9
Human Figure, portrait 128-33

I

Imagination 92
Impressionists 14
Inspiration 20

K

Klimt, Gustav 16
Kolinsky sable brushes 36

L

Laying a flat wash 46
Laying a graded wash 47
Lead pencils 39
Léger, Fernand 16
Leopard 98-105
Light over dark 53, 61
Light to dark 70, 91, 106
Liquid acrylic paints 63

M

Magazines as inspiration 20
Mantegna, Andrea 14
Mixed media 56
Mondrian, Piet 14, 86, 92
Moore, Henry 13
Museums 96, 106

N

Natural bristle brushes 36
Natural hair brushes 36
Negative shapes 67
Neutral tones 27-8
Non-spill water pot 39
NOT paper 34

O

Oblique perspective 24
Op Art 16
Opacity 33, 53, 60, 108, 134
Orley, Pieter Van 13
Orley, Richard Van 12, 13
Overlaying washes 49, 108
Ox hair brushes 36

P

Painting wet-in-wet 50
Paints 32-3
Palettes 39
Papers 34-5
        stretching 42-3
Parallel Perspective 24
Pencils 39
Perspective 24, 25, 70, 76
Photographic reference 20, 58, 98, 134
Picasso, Pablo 13, 15, 92
Piper, John 16, 17
Planning your picture 22-5
Plastic palettes 39
Plato 22
Pollock, Jackson 84
Portraits 128-33
Postcards 62
Poussin, Gaspard 13
Poussin, Nicolas 13
Precipitated chalk 32
Primary colours 26-7
Pure watercolour 70, 91, 106

R

Rag-rolling 54
Ready-stretched paper 42
Recommended brushes 37
Renaissance 22-4
Riley, Bridget 13, 16, 17
Rolling 65
Rooftops 76-83
Rossetti, Dante Gabriel 14
Rough paper 34
Round brushes 36
Rubens, Peter Paul 13
Rulers 55

S

Sable brushes 36
Safari parks 96
Sandby, Paul 13
Scene from Another World 92-5
Sceptre Gold brushes 37
Schiele, Egon 13, 16
Scumbling 60, 136
Secondary colours 26-7
Series 7 brushes 37, 124
Sketchbook 20, 58, 92
Sketching 96
Skin tones 126, 128
Sponges 42-3
Squirrel brushes 36
Staining 33
Straight lines 55
Stretching paper 42-3, 46
Stuffed animals 106
Sunflowers 62-7
Supports 34-5
Surrealism 16
Sutherland, Graham 16, 17
Synthetic fibre brushes 36

T

Table easel 39
Tempera 12
Tertiary colours 26
Texture 54, 77
The Bathers 134-9
Thumbnail sketch 135
Tone, adjusting by diluting 44-5, 71
        adjusting by overlaying 49, 108
        gradation 47, 51

Toning colours down 88
Tracing paper 98
Tulips 114-17
Turner, J.M.W. 28
Understanding colour 26-9
Uneven colour 103

V

Vaillant, Le 13
Vanishing point 24
Vase of flowers 114
Viewpoint 24, 25

W

Warm colours 28
Washes 46-7, 49, 71, 73, 79, 87, 107,
        115, 135-6
        overlaying 49
Water pots 39
Watercolour papers see Supports
Weight of paper 34
Wet-in-wet 50-1, 78
Wet-on-dry 52, 72

Y

Yorkshire Dales 58-61

Z

Zoos 96, 98

CAFÉ · FRANÇAIS · TRADITIONNEL

─ W·S·GRANDISON ─